SHIT LIFE TO SELF-MADE

A Real Talk Roadmap for the Lost and Ambitious

JANI HAVUNEN

ISBN **978-9-52881-154-1** (pbk)
ISBN **978-9-52881-153-4** (hcv)
ISBN **978-9-52881-155-8** (ebook)

This book doesn't sell hope—it earns it. Jani Havunen writes with a level of honesty that feels both rare and necessary, turning survival into self-understanding without shortcuts or clichés.
Aaron Poynton | Author, Bestselling Author, *Think Like A Black Sheep*

I appreciated how the book refuses to blame the past while still taking it seriously. That balance is rare and refreshing.
Alex Melen | Co-Founder, SmartSites

A brutal but compassionate look at survival mode, Jani explains how trauma shapes decisions in ways that finally made sense to me.
Bryan Howard | CEO of Peoplyst, Author of *The Vanguard Edge*

This isn't motivation—it's orientation. The book helped me understand why I felt lost, and how to move without pretending I had a map.
Casel Burnett | Vice President, LODI, and International Bestselling Author of *No Regrets*

This felt less like a memoir and more like a guide written from the inside, quietly reassuring for anyone still searching.
Shawn Johal | Business Growth Coach, Elevation Leaders, Bestselling Author of *The Happy Leader*

This book doesn't glorify rock bottom—it explains it. And in doing so, it makes change feel possible rather than miraculous.
Tamara Nall | CEO & Founder, The Leading Niche

Instead of blaming the past, Jani Havunen teaches you how to make sense of it. That shift alone makes this book worth reading.
Trissa Tismal-Capili | USA Today and Wall Street Journal Bestselling Author

After reading Mr. Jani's book, I was awestruck that we've travelled similar treacherous life paths, in different spheres of the world literally in tandem the journeys. After some personal serious soul searching I found his book will provide the reader who is currently at various points of life's struggles pushing themselves to seek and propel themselves over the finish line and be inspired to complete the fight for true success and happiness no matter what the adversity that they're facing. Bravo Jani and continued success motivating and inspiring the world.
Darius Ross | Managing Director, D Alexander Ross Real Estate Capital Partners Interest LLC

Dedication

To my family—the truest foundation I have ever known.

In memory of Mr. Damien and Pulla—your loyalty and love will always live in my heart.

To our new family members, the French Bulldogs Mr. Reddington and Prada—your joy, energy, and companionship remind me daily of life's simple treasures.

To my wife, Riina—my partner, my strength, and my home. Your unwavering belief in me has given me the courage to keep moving forward.

To my friends and all those who walked with me along the way— thank you for your honesty, presence, and for reminding me that no one succeeds alone.

And to everyone who crossed my path, in light or in shadow—you were part of the story that shaped me. For that, I am grateful.

Foreword

My name is Kari, and I've been a friend of the author for well over ten years. I have also had the privilege of being a witness to this transformation.

When I first crossed paths with Jani, we did not end up as friends. This was a few years before the transformation and change began. That first encounter was not an everyday experience – it was like a tornado rushing into my office and exiting at the same speed, leaving me wondering what had just happened.

It could easily be said, with a blink of irony, that a first impression is not everything when it comes to the beginning of a true friendship.

This book is a mental portrait of a small boy struggling through life, from childhood trauma into adulthood. Not knowing the real methods to create a solid foundation for the future led to poor decisions and an identity built like an upside-down pyramid – fast-forwarding through life without caring about the conse-quences of actions, or even about life itself.

In today's world, a reckless lifestyle and substance abuse are often only symptoms of untreated mental disorders or unresolved childhood trauma. Facing trauma, or any deeply uncomfortable feelings, is always hard and often leads to avoidance – pulling you back into the same cycle again and again.

From my own experience with PTSD, I have recognized the impor-tance of guidance and support in understanding trauma. Reading encouraging stories based on real-life experiences can be crucial. When you have peer support, explanations of brain chemistry, and psychological insight, you gain tools to begin processing and reflecting on your own path. This can be the key to meaningful change in your life.

This book does not focus on mistakes as failures. Instead, they are presented as reflections on behavior, helping the reader understand the real reasons behind it. How do you break patterns? How do you handle emotions? Facing what's inside is difficult, but it is also rewarding. Every lived moment matters – and when processed correctly, it may even become your strength in the future.

Jani's life has been marked by survival, chaos, and struggle in many forms until change began to rise, piece by piece. It is fair to say that there has been a previous life and a present life, with a long and demanding process of transformation between them.

His exceptional memory of past events and his ability to understand his own mental state – even during psychosis – create a clear and compelling narrative from chaos toward change. The book explores how everything started, what led to transformation, and whether anything meaningful could be carried forward from the past.

Reclaiming ownership of his life, earning a master's degrees, and becoming a successful entrepreneur stand as proof that change is real.

If your life feels out of your control – if you are searching or lost – this book is for you.

Kari Almen
Friend and believer

Table of Contents

Note to the Reader

The neuroscientific and psychological descriptions in this book are based on widely available research, popular science sources, and the author's own observations and lived experience. These perspectives are used as narrative tools to make sense of internal mental states and life events as they were understood in retrospect.

The descriptions are intentionally simplified and interpretive in nature. They are not intended to offer a comprehensive, clinical, or scientific account of brain function or mental health conditions. This book is not a medical or scientific work, but a personal narrative in which scientific language is used to illuminate lived experience.

Preface

I began my first "book" when I was about eight years old, typing with small fingers on an old machine that clattered louder than my thoughts. I never finished that project, and the message would have been very different back then. Looking back now, I believe a small author has lived inside me ever since—quietly observing, collecting, and waiting for the right moment to speak.

That moment is now.

This book was not born from theory, study, or the safety of distance. It was born from lived experience—hard, messy, painful experience that shaped me long before I understood its impact. Much of my life unfolded as a series of battles in the dark: addiction, loneliness, shame, crime, survival mode, and seasons when I no longer cared whether I lived or died. I walked those roads mostly alone—sometimes by choice, often because I did not know any other way.

The purpose of this book is simple: so that others do not have to walk that road alone.

Throughout the years, I learned how our minds, shaped by childhood, trauma, and the environments we grow up in, quietly directs our emotions, reactions, beliefs, and behaviors. I learned how easily survival replaces strategy, how quickly shame becomes identity, and how hard it is to heal wounds you cannot name. I also learned that change is possible—slow, uneven, humbling, but possible. Every rock bottom carries a pivot point, even if you cannot see it at the time.

This is not a story written to blame anyone, including myself. I spent years trying to do that—assigning fault, replaying memories, and clinging to bitterness—but none of it changed anything. The past is fixed. What we can change is how we understand it and how we move forward from it. My hope is that these pages can act as a mirror for you, a companion, or a spark—something that helps you reflect on your own journey.

If you have felt lost, this book is for you.

If you have felt broken, this book is for you.

If you have felt alone in your struggles, this book is for you.

If you are still searching for meaning, direction, or peace, I wrote this so you know that transformation is not reserved for the lucky—it is possible for anyone willing to confront their truth.

This is my story.

But more importantly, this is a message: your story matters, too.
– Jani Havunen

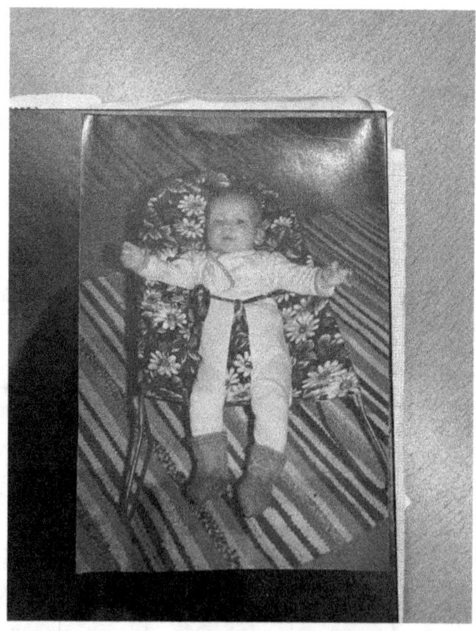

Me at the stage when everything was about to begin.

PART ONE

THE LONG ROAD TO NOWHERE

CHAPTER 1

Leaving Before I Knew Where I Was Going

The Decision to Leave Home at 15

In this book, as I describe my childhood and the events that have shaped my life and analyze how things might have turned out differently, I am not blaming anyone, including myself, for what happened. Of course, at one time I did, but during my journey, I realized that dwelling on the past or assigning blame will not change it. We live in the present and can make decisions that influence the future, but the past is fixed, so we must learn from it. The aim of this book is to stimulate your thinking and awaken your reflections. Use it as a mirror and a spark for your inner fire.

Do you remember your first memory of this world? I do. I was three years old when I woke in the house that served as my home for the first five years of my life. The awakening itself was not pleasant: I had soiled my pants during the night. That home was in the small western Finnish town of Kihniö.

Living under the same roof were my grandparents, my mother, my three uncles—one of whom had a wife and two children—and me. Fortunately, the house was spacious; otherwise, I might also have grown up claustrophobic. In size and composition, our household was rather different from what is usually called "normal."

Nevertheless, I had a wonderful time playing with my cousins, and the rural setting was a perfect place to begin life. In the countryside, people connect more deeply with nature; so did I, especially when I joined one of my uncles on hunting and fishing trips. He became an important figure to me because I did not have my biological father in my life and still do not. My uncle partly filled that role by taking me along and, above all, spending time with me. That is what a child needs from the adults—usually the parents—in addition to clear limits and unconditional love.

My mother was only twenty-one when she had me, so she was still quite young herself, and my upbringing became a communal project of sorts. I have many fond memories of that first home, as well as some less pleasant ones. Often, I fell asleep to the steady, calming sound of my grandmother's asthma nebulizer, which was like a lullaby. A darker memory is that the uncle I admired drank heavily. He did not behave badly otherwise, but he was often away from home for weeks at a time, and each absence made the little boy in me anxious.

When I was about five, my mother found new love, and we moved to a nearby, slightly larger town called Parkano. We went from one rural area to another, which was no hardship. My new household consisted of my mother, my stepfather, a few of his children from a previous marriage, and me. Three of them were older than I, and one was younger, so again I found myself in a family arrangement quite unlike what I had known.

One advantage of the move was that my elementary school was only three hundred meters from our house. There were only two pupils in my class, so the teaching was highly personal. I also became fascinated by computers and games at an early age. My first machine was a Commodore 64. Later, I had a Nintendo 8-bit, an Amiga 500, and eventually my first PC, a 486 SX-25.

Computers intrigued me. I loved dismantling PCs and putting them back together. Playing games such as Leisure Suit Larry with an English dictionary at my side sharpened both my language and problem-solving skills. I was a good student in elementary school, and thanks to those games, my English marks were consistently nine or ten on Finland's grading scale—even though I knew nothing about effective study techniques, my average was above eight in grades 1–6. I was not gifted at drawing and sometimes envied my classmate Jarkko, who was.

In lower secondary school (grades 7–9), peer pressure and the desire for social approval began to overwhelm me. Self-esteem, which develops critically between ages seven and twelve, also played a part. When a young person craves acceptance, he may do rather foolish things that seem perfectly reasonable at the time. To fit in, I started smoking and occasionally misbehaving to amuse others, which earned me detentions and other penalties. I did not realize then that what I sought was simply acceptance from my peers.

During upper elementary school, alcohol also entered my life. Environmental pressure, peer influence, and the example set by the adults around me all played a part. It is worth noting, though, that people differ: one of my friends has never tasted alcohol, cigarettes, or drugs. He says he has always viewed them as unhealthy, and I can hardly disagree. If alcohol were invented today, it would certainly be classified as a drug.

By this time, I was already adrift. My self-esteem—damaged by upheaval and uncertainty—left me unsure of who I was. Fortunately, illicit drugs were rare at my school.

I first became drunk at about twelve. The experience was neither spectacular nor what I had imagined. I spent a lot of time with slightly older cousins, and from a child's perspective, our escapades felt exciting.

Even so, I completed upper elementary school with an average below eight, despite courting acceptance through foolish behavior and despite the toxic climate at home. The adults drank heavily and fought. I remember lying in my room while screams, shouts, and the sounds of physical violence passed straight through the walls. My stepfather never hit me, but the psychological damage was severe. Trying to broker peace among drunken adults was anything but easy for a child.

Once, when I was about ten, the adults were drinking and arguing downstairs. Sitting in my room, I picked up a souvenir knife from a family trip to Lapland and wondered whether cutting my wrists might help. A voice inside me said, *"Jani, do not even think about this."* I set the knife aside and pushed the thought away.

The worst thing about that environment was the lack of safety. When a child grows up without a basic sense of security—and without adults who filter events and explain what is happening—it is hardly surprising that his mental wiring slips off the normal grid.

Back in Kihniö, I was never part of a typical father-mother-child family; I belonged to a community. Even then, I felt like an outsider, though I could not have articulated it. I also could not understand why I had no father.

After we moved to Parkano, two of my stepfather's older children no longer lived at home, but two still did. My mother and step-father then had two boys of their own. They are legally my step-brothers, but I consider them brothers. We are seven and thirteen years apart, and our relationship have always been good.

My stepfather favored his own children. I worked around the house but received no reward, so I turned to food—and the dopa-mine it releases—for comfort. No one taught me that you can earn by doing; this omission later colored my attitude towards money and reinforced unhelpful habits. The unstable environment also influenced my growing dopamine hunger.

Once again, I was the outsider in my own home, a feeling that has shaped my emotions and behavior for decades.

When I was twelve, the uncle who had been so important to me died. I was upstairs in my room when I heard my mother answer the phone and begin to cry. She came up to tell me the news, and it felt as if my world collapsed in seconds.

Through my tears, I suddenly remembered a dream from the previous night: two white horses pulled a white sleigh in which my uncle sat, flying toward the sky. He waved and smiled at me.

They found him sitting on the toilet seat; he had died of a heart attack. The autopsy later revealed three blockages in his heart. My grandmother told me he had been taking my grandfather's heart medication—without permission—and had never gone to a doctor. People often neglect their own health, and tragedies follow. Later that same year, my grandfather also passed away.

In the 1990s, there was little information—or conversation—about grief, so neither I nor the adults around me knew how to process my sorrow. The death of someone so important left a trauma that stayed in my psyche for decades.

When I recall my childhood, the strongest thread is the feeling of being an outsider. Poor self-esteem made me unsure of myself, and that insecurity shaped my later life. Being unsure meant that I doubted and underestimated myself, creating mental barriers— beliefs about who I was. I started to engage in negative self-talk. This had severe consequences for many decades to come.

Because I lacked proper guidance and encouragement, I was already adrift. I remember enrolling in a karate class with my older cousins when I was ten. I felt frightened and unsure of how I would perform or what sort of feedback I would receive. Such anxiety is common when a child grows up without consistent, constructive feedback or a truly safe environment; it seeps straight into one's emotions, confidence, and thought patterns.

Before I describe leaving home at fifteen, let me quickly summarize the key points.

If I Were to Talk to My Younger Self

Learn From the Past, Don't Dwell on It

The past is fixed, and no amount of blame—toward others or yourself—will change it. What matters is learning from it and choosing differently in the present. Your story is not an excuse; it is raw material for growth.

Your First Memories Shaped You, but Did Not Define You

I know you remember waking up in that first house in Kihniö at three years old, embarrassed because you had soiled yourself. That memory may have felt shameful, but it was only the beginning of a long story. What matters is not how it started, but how you use it.

A Childhood Without a Father Doesn't Make You Less

You missed having a father, and it made you feel like an outsider. But you had people who stepped in—your uncle, your grandparents—and the time spent with them planted seeds of resilience. You didn't know it then, but being different would later become your strength.

Safe Environments Matter

You grew up in households filled with instability, violence, and unfairness. That lack of safety wired your brain to seek comfort in food, alcohol, and later, other escapes. It wasn't weakness—it was survival. But it also left scars you would need to rewire later.

Early School Years Showed Your Potential

Even in the chaos, you shone. Computers, languages, problem-solving—you loved learning without even knowing it was learning. Those skills stayed with you and later became tools for rebuilding your life.

Peer Pressure Stole Your Confidence

In lower secondary school, you chased approval, started smoking, and tried to be funny by misbehaving. What you wanted was simple: to belong. You didn't yet know that true belonging starts from within, not from what others think of you.

Alcohol Was Never the Answer

At twelve, you got drunk for the first time. You thought it was exciting, but it wasn't. It was another escape. Later, it became a trap. Remember this: alcohol never gave you freedom—it only borrowed your peace and charged interest.

The Pain of Violence and Fear

Hearing adults fight, lying awake listening to screams, and trying to broker peace as a child—these moments carved deep wounds. They left you feeling unsafe in your own home. That lack of safety is why you struggled with trust later on.

Darkness and a Knife at Ten Years Old

I know there was a moment when you thought about ending it all, sitting with that knife in your hand. But even then, a voice inside you told you not to do it. That voice was your future—the proof that you were meant for more.

Grief That Was Never Processed

The deaths of your uncle and grandfather left holes in your heart that no one helped you fill. In those days, grief wasn't talked about. But your sorrow was real, and it shaped you. Those unspoken feelings became heavy baggage you carried for years.

The Outsider Feeling

At home, you felt like an outsider—always less than, always on the margins. That feeling chipped away at your self-esteem and gave birth to negative self-talk. You believed lies about yourself:

that you weren't enough, that you didn't belong. Those beliefs became barriers you would later need to break.

Anxiety Was Never Your Fault

When you walked into karate class at ten years old, you were already anxious—not because you were weak, but because no one had ever taught you how to feel safe in your own skin. That anxiety was learned from your environment, not part of who you are.

What Freedom Felt Like and What It Cost

In the summer of 1995, we found a pleasant house in the center of Parkano. I had finished lower secondary school and was about to start upper secondary school. I had no idea what I wanted to do with my life—which is quite normal at that age.

Moving out on my own and escaping a stressful home environment felt wonderful. Still, the change had an unintended downside: with no adults around, I suddenly had no boundaries. Every weekend, my flat turned into a party for all teenagers—and some slightly older youths—who hung around the town center at night. A salesperson from the Shell gas station opposite my flat even joked that all the teenagers were at Jani's place, leaving the usual hangouts deserted.

Hosting the local party hub made me feel important. I was "popular" because everyone wanted access to my flat. Yet the absence of limits quickly affected my schooling: my grades in upper secondary began to slip. I was not motivated to do homework or study, so I dropped into the part-time evening stream. A young person needs structure to create stability and a basic sense of safety— things I had lacked all my life.

My friends and I had a blast; the flat became a weekend club, and before long, even adults joined in. The whole town talked about the teenager hosting constant parties. Once or twice, my mother and stepfather staged surprise raids—quite a sight, especially when my mother screamed at friends crawling out of the back door.

Alcohol never suited me. I drank huge amounts, and my behavior turned strange and aggressive–though I was usually so drunk that serious physical harm was unlikely. Verbal harm was another matter. After one party, a girl I knew asked whether I remembered anything from the night before (I did not). She told me she had fought another girl while I stood by yelling, "Kill that bitch!"–cheering on her opponent. I was mortified and apologized; she forgave me eventually, but it took time. Episodes like that were common, and I often ended up crying for no clear reason.

Sober, I was sensitive and kind, but no one–including me–suggested I should stop drinking. In our society, people prefer to gossip when the subject is absent, but that helps no one. Constructive feedback, delivered kindly, can steer a person in a better direction–if he is willing to listen.

After a year, the landlord evicted me; my rent was often late, and the constant parties annoyed the neighbors. I knew nothing about handling money. No one had taught me–nor ever rewarded me–for work. I came from a poor background in both assets and emotional security. However, I did not yet realize that these hardships would later fuel my transformation.

Once again, I was an outsider–in the middle of a "community" that loved my flat as a party venue. People tried to please me to keep the doors open. Apart from my mother and two older cousins, I saw little of my extended family. Years later, I heard that one of my godmothers had left a Christmas calendar at my door, but I never met her; perhaps that was her way of showing she cared.

By 1997, I had moved to my fourth home, another flat nearby–smaller, thankfully, so the large-scale parties stopped, although my weekend drinking did not. Life calmed a little. I spent time with my cousins Janne and Juha and our friend Kalle, who lived in the same building. We played Dungeons & Dragons, RuneQuest,

Cyberpunk, and LAN games like Warcraft and Doom. It felt exciting and good.

At Vaasa's Ranta Rock festival in 1998, a friend and I ordered so many Hot Shots at the hotel bar that they ran out of the liqueur. I blacked out—as usual. Apparently, a minor Finnish celebrity hesitated to drink a flaming shot, so I grabbed him by the throat and said, "If you order it on flames, you drink it on flames." More shameful behavior. At festivals from 1995 to 1998, I often drank until I collapsed and crawled through the mud; waking up in wet, filthy clothes became routine.

Back then, I never reflected on my behavior. I drank as if I were trying to drown unrecognized sorrow and trauma. Why did I change so completely when drunk? I will analyze this later on.

My poor self-esteem manifested in many ways. I was ashamed of my body—an asymmetrical self-image kept me from using saunas or public showers, branding me as peculiar and deepening my trauma. I worried constantly that people would laugh at me and mock my appearance. I felt profoundly uncomfortable.

Between 1998 and 1999, I worked in a computer shop. I loved computers so much that I often slept at the store, repairing machines and gaming through the night. Games can be addictive; the brain craves their rewards, and so did mine. I enrolled in evening high school but soon dropped out again—computers were far more appealing. I did not realize that this passion, too, was beginning to control my life—driven by a craving for dopamine that did nothing to heal the underlying wound in my psyche.

In 1999, I began my military service, lost thirty kilos, and became fit, revealing how out of shape I had been. During my service, a friend, also named Jani, died in a motorcycle accident only ten kilometers from home. Life can feel brutally unfair.

Released from the army, I slipped back into poor eating and heavy drinking; ignorance about nutrition and training, plus near-weekly alcohol binges, meant I regained all the lost weight and more. Moreover, I had no normal relationships with girls–many peers did, but my poor self-esteem and an unhealthy bond with my mother distorted my thinking and behavior. I did not see it then.

I had a few brief relationships with women, but whenever a partner wanted to move on–or was simply not that interested–I clung to her and behaved in self-destructive ways. I did not realize it then, but this reaction grew out of childhood trauma, an unhealthy attachment to my mother, and self-esteem–a deep-seated fear of losing people.

I remember the thoughts running through my head; I wallowed in self-pity, convinced that my world would collapse if she left. The early loss of an important figure and a lifelong sense of being an outsider were probably the main forces at work in my subconscious. Could those symptoms have been treated? Possibly–but only if someone, including me, had recognized them. Even a caring listener, professional or not, might have made a difference.

In 2000, my life changed again when I fell in with a new crowd. As in my earlier school years, I unconsciously adopted risky behavior to earn respect and acceptance. Faulty self-esteem, built on shaky foundations, can lead to real trouble: my first conviction came in 2001.

Freedom without boundaries set me adrift. Had I had someone to talk to–someone who truly understood my situation–it might have changed the course of events. With a trusted listener, we might have recognized my need for healing and been able to act. So, make sure you find at least one person with whom you can share part of your life. Reflect, and become aware.

I cannot yet tally the full cost of this "freedom." An unstable upbringing pushed me out on my own, and the choices that followed carried a heavy price. Whether something positive would emerge remained to be seen.

If I Were to Talk to My Younger Self

Freedom Without Boundaries Is a Trap

Moving out early may feel liberating, but without guidance or structure, independence can quickly spiral into chaos—parties replace purpose, and school, finances, and health fall apart.

Structure Equals Safety

Teenagers thrive on routines and clear expectations; these provide stability, motivation, and peace of mind. Without them, the ground beneath you feels shaky, no matter how free you think you are.

Unhealed Pain Always Looks for an Escape

Alcohol, endless gaming, and reckless behavior often mask deeper wounds, such as trauma or low self-worth. These "coping mechanisms" only push healing further away.

Alcohol Changes More Than Feelings

Alcohol does not just change how you feel—it can change who you are. Intoxication breeds aggression, blackouts, and regret, damaging both friendships and self-image. If no one steps in, the cycle deepens.

Money Matters More Than It Seems

Poor financial habits—never learned, never taught—can snowball into rent arrears, debt, and eviction. Financial literacy is freedom in its truest form.

Popularity Built on Convenience Is Fragile

Popularity built on what you provide—access, parties, attention—is fragile. When the fun stops, so do the "friends," leaving you lonelier than before. Real connection is built on respect, not convenience.

Shame Feeds Isolation

Hiding flaws, whether in body image or personality, only magnifies anxiety and self-contempt. Self-acceptance is the first step toward belonging.

Temporary Turnarounds Are Not Enough

Discipline and success in short bursts—whether in the army, sports, or studies—collapse without addressing the root causes: self-worth, attachment wounds, and the fear of abandonment.

Relationships Reflect Your Inner World

If you cling too tightly or fear being left, it is often because of scars left by early losses or unmet needs. Healing those wounds changes how you love.

A Young Person Needs a Trusted Listener

Most importantly, a young person needs at least one trusted listener: someone who sees the signs, hears your story without judgment, and reminds you that you matter. That single connection can redirect an entire life.

The Cost of Unguided Freedom

The truth is simple: freedom without guidance comes at a high cost. Healing begins with self-awareness—and with the courage to seek out those who will listen, support, and remind you of your worth.

CHAPTER 2

Walking Without a Map

Life in Motion, Without a Destination

My first conviction was for drunk driving. I received a suspended sentence of a few months and a fine. It happened in the parking lot of the local gas station: I had driven to a bar, and after closing time, I got behind the wheel and headed for the station. The attendants called the police, and I spent the night in a cell before being charged.

Looking back, I feel like an idiot. At the time, though, the incident fed my ego. I wanted not only external applause but also an inner thrill: You did it—you broke the rules and survived. Genuine self-efficacy should come from success in sports, study, work, or real self-development, not from committing crimes.

Why did breaking the law feel good? I had absorbed the values of the crowd I mixed with. Directionless people are easily molded, and I was steering myself. No one urged me to drive drunk; I manipulated myself into it.

When you accept a group's rules, you earn rewards—both internal and external—for following them. Disobedience brings neither praise nor pleasure and may even invite punishment. Positive feedback triggers dopamine, making you feel good, and tightening group cohesion.

The same mechanism explains my antics at school: I amused myself and others to harvest those dopamine hits.

Why did I seek out such groups? A chronic sense of being an outsider pushed me recklessly forward. I craved excitement, adrenaline, and ego boosts. I never realized my life was moving without a destination—and heading for catastrophe.

By the time of my first conviction, I was already drifting; the verdict altered the drift's direction. My relationship with money was equally faulty. I came from a poor background, had no financial skills, and coupled with an addictive mind, created a toxic mix.

I first stepped into a gym at thirteen, went a few times, then quit until I was about twenty. I idolized men with big muscles, hoping they would patch my fragile self-esteem, so I began using anabolic steroids—another disastrous decision, as I will explain later.

In 2002, drugs entered my life. Friends were already using, and I started with cannabis. Food tasted heavenly, films seemed brilliant, and everyone was hilarious.

Next came amphetamine. Two minutes after snorting a line from a CD cover in a car, I felt energized and powerful. Later, I added prescription pills to help me sleep. My cocktail now included steroids, street drugs, medication, and plenty of alcohol.

My emotional life had been off track before; these substances pushed it further off the rails. Even on alcohol alone, I had vandalized property and picked fights I usually lost. Drugs deepened the wound. Binges sometimes lasted days in a shuttered flat. Amphetamine calmed me at first, but eventually, it triggered something like psychosis—a topic I will explore later.

My next conviction came in 2002. It involved drugs, economic crimes, assault, and destruction of property—this one I served by community service. When we look at the crimes that I committed, we can see the direction my life was heading.

A crucial part of healthy self-esteem is the ability to handle setbacks, but with my background, you can only imagine how that went. So, the cloud over my mind was forging itself, as I behaved recklessly, and the spiral of bad habits and actions continued.

In 2003, I was convicted of a firearm offense and destruction of property and was sentenced to community service. In 2004, most of my community service was converted to jail time, after I was caught forging my medical certificate. I did not participate in the community service for any solid reason, so I tried a shortcut—but failed.

I went to jail for the first time in 2005 and served about nine months. After I was released, one of my longtime friends picked me up, and the party started again. Our Midsummer Festival in 2006 felt like a blast: amphetamine (which I had arranged on the way home) and, of course, plenty of alcohol.

In 2007, I moved to Tampere, but first I spent one chaotic month working as a security officer in Ibiza. I had already done a few gigs in Helsinki in 2004-2005, but Ibiza was another level. Any time I was not on duty, I was drinking and snorting cocaine with my coworkers. We also took sleeping pills—though we never went to bed. One colleague told me it would be his first and last shift with us; chasing an imaginary fairy-tale creature around the apartment while half-conscious was not his idea of fun.

After Ibiza, I drifted, living an unstable life filled with various drugs, alcohol, and anabolic steroids. At times, it felt like a movie, but in reality, I was burning the candle at both ends. There were funny moments, but my body and mind paid the price.

While working as a bouncer in 2007, I tore a chest muscle separating two men in a bar fight. The hospital decided to "leave it as it is" and recheck in a few months—an error. When they finally scanned it, surgery was unavoidable. I had the first operation in a private clinic, but when I woke up, the surgeons told me I would need a second operation because of excess fluid. After they put me under again, I vomited into my lungs—about 1.5 liters if I recall correctly—and woke up in intensive care on IV antibiotics and strong painkillers. Life can be short, so remember to live it.

In 2009, I received my next conviction: forgery, fraud, gross fraud, aggravated payment fraud, aggravated drug offense, tax fraud, registration offense, and illegal importation—one year and nine months in prison. The list was so "versatile" that local authorities nicknamed me "the Tinkerer." Another nickname was "Balloon," from surveillance photos in 2008-2009, when I weighed about 147 kg. My body and mind were under immense pressure. In 2010, I lost about 42 kilograms, and my veins were grateful.

I went to jail again in 2011 and was released in December 2012. During these two sentences, I exercised, but that was about the only sensible thing available. I avoided drugs and steroids the second time. I got myself in good physical shape also during this conviction, but it faded shortly after my release.

After release, I kept drifting—drugs, steroids, alcohol, and the so-called underworld. By then, I had abused various substances for roughly twelve years. Add stress and little sleep, and the results appeared: several psychotic episodes. In 2014, friends had me admitted to a mental hospital.

The first night, they placed me in a round room with cameras for observation. Walking the corridors, I seemed almost normal compared with other patients. One thought he was a pixie; another walked around silently with his hand held out. My room-mate looked unpredictable, but I turned my back, slept—and survived.

This was not my first visit to that hospital: in 2013, I visited the Finnish singer Jippu there, an event she mentions in her book *Jippu—When the Butterfly Stops Breathing*.

I was discharged after a few days. One main trigger for the psychosis was severe sleep deprivation. Once I caught up on sleep, I felt terrible—not physically, but socially and emotionally. With a clear mind, I understood what had happened. A friend said, bluntly but kindly, "Jani, your psyche can't handle any more substances." I appreciated the honesty, but I was not ready to quit.

In December 2013, I met Riina, though I did not yet know she would become my wife. We started dating in the summer of 2014 and became a couple that September. I also met Riina's enormous Rottweiler, Mr. Damien, and her sister's French bulldog, Pulla—now a fourteen-year-old grandma as I write this. She passed away during this project. Riina and I got engaged on May 1 2015. A healthy relationship would prove crucial to my transformation, as I will explain later.

Because of earlier economic crimes (2008-2011), I was convicted in 2015 for aiding aggravated tax fraud: two years in prison. I began that sentence in 2016.

During that stretch, something shifted deep inside. No one told me to change; I could not stand the life—and the things people did to each other—anymore. I began studying in my cell, starting with a high school psychology book. Fascinated, I applied everything to my own life. With the help of the prison's student advisor (once I insisted on my rights), I joined a mathematics course taught by a nearby high school teacher—no small feat in a closed prison.

I earned a good grade, then completed more math and psychology courses in my cell. In early 2017, I transferred to an open prison and officially enrolled in high school.

A few words about the system: Finnish prisons vary, and many inmates have no desire to change, so staff attitudes are often negative. One official's parting "motivation" to me was, "Jani, let's aim for you not to come back within three years." Eight years have passed.

Mental health issues are widespread yet rarely identified or treated. Substance abuse is often a form of self-medication—my case included. Lock someone in a box for a few years, and do not expect them to emerge cured. But you also have the opportunity to do meaningful things, such as studying. For that, I am grateful.

I was released on June 22, 2017 with an ankle monitor; a few months later, they removed it, and I was finally free. By then, I had spent about four years in prison. Note that a person can certainly use their time better in general.

Between 2000 and 2017, I experienced speed, danger, comedy, and horror on both sides of society. I felt that I was in the middle of something I did not belong in, and seeing how people treated each other in the underworld was one driver for my change. I have also witnessed oddities in the so-called normal world. Still, this book is meant to motivate, not criticize, so let us keep moving toward inspiration.

In the coming chapters, I will delve into my mind and reflect on what has happened to me over the years.

If I Were to Talk to My Younger Self

Thrill Is Only a Counterfeit of Real Achievement

You will chase adrenaline and applause because you do not yet have genuine wins in sport, study, or work. But the buzz will fade fast, and it will push you into ever-riskier stunts to feel alive.

Values Are Contagious

With no clear direction of your own, you will absorb the unwritten rules of whatever crowd you are in—and you will even reward yourself for following them. Be careful whose approval you chase.

Addiction Masks, Then Magnifies Pain

Addiction will first mask, then magnify, the pain of feeling like an outsider. Drugs, alcohol, and steroids might numb insecurity and give you instant belonging, but each dose deepens the hole you are trying to fill.

Financial Ignorance Becomes a Prison Sentence

Financial ignorance mixed with impulsivity will lead you down dangerous paths. Growing up poor and untrained in money management, you will treat fraud like a shortcut to success—until those shortcuts take you straight to prison.

Neglecting Your Body Will Sabotage Your Mind

Steroids, sleepless nights, and untreated injuries will strain your health and prime you for psychosis. Remember: mental stability begins with the basics—sleep, nutrition, and self-care.

Prison Can Punish You or Pivot You

Prison can either punish you or pivot you. What makes the difference is how you choose to use the time. Exercise and self-directed study can transform inactive time into discovery, giving you a new identity no one can take away.

Sleep Is Non-Negotiable

A psychotic break will come after days of stimulants and insomnia. Your brain needs rest as desperately as your lungs need air.

Honest Allies Change Everything

A blunt friend, a loving partner, and—even two loyal dogs—will give you the mirror and motivation your ego alone never could.

Systems Will Fail You Without Mental Health Care

Most inmates carry untreated disorders, and locking people up without therapy stores the problem for later release. You will see this firsthand.

You Can Own Your Story

But here is the biggest truth: you can own your story. By turning chaos into a narrative with meaning, you stop being a passenger in your own life and finally become its author.

Survival over Strategy

The door clicked shut behind me, and for the first time in fifteen years, there were no adults on the other side. A single bulb buzzed above the kitchenette. The refrigerator sighed when I opened it: one half-empty ketchup bottle, sweaty cheese slices stuck to wax paper, two cans of beer.

I pulled a chair to the window and watched neon from the Shell station smear across wet pavement. From somewhere downtown came the muffled thump of bass–other people's Friday night.

Inside the flat, the silence was thick enough to taste–no grandmother's wheezy nebulizer, no stepfather's slurred threats. I should have felt free. Instead, my pulse rattled in my ears like a locked door I had forgotten to prop open. *Now what?* That question lasted ten seconds before I cracked the first beer.

I can still remember the sour taste and sharp smell of cheap beer. At the same time, I had a twofold flashback. The first was of the night I sat in my room at home with the souvenir knife, listening to the sounds of a fight. The second was from my childhood, in my first home in Kihniö, when my uncle woke me up before we left on a hunting trip.

I no longer had to listen to the sounds of fighting–I was free. Was this the same feeling I had with my uncle on that beautiful morning in Kihniö? I felt free but also empty. No, it was not the same. I was alone. I was confused, happy, and sad all at once.

I had no rules, but I also had no real safety net. My mother visited regularly, so in that sense, she had not left. She did her best under those circumstances. Still, I was a little boy alone in a big world. Every night, as I went to bed, I wondered what would happen next. I remember riding a roller coaster of emotions almost every single night. I was lost and alone.

If we imagine a situation where the gas light is on in a car and the range is only twenty kilometers, and then compare that to a gas station's full fuel reserve, we can get some idea of what my situation was like back then. I had to survive with the equivalent of a twenty-kilometer range. In contrast, under normal circumstances, I would have had the full reserve of a gas station—a proper strategy.

Squirrels can starve in trees full of nuts if they panic and hoard the wrong ones. I, too, picked the wrong nuts many times—but I survived. There were many situations where the opposite could have happened.

Only after several decades did I realize that most of my actions were driven by survival mode. There was no strategy—not even the idea that a strategy could exist. My only goal was to survive.

I have described my relationship with money earlier. Money played a major role in my survival-based way of living. I remember it as if it were yesterday when my first landlord said to me, "Jani, this is now the third time we've had this same discussion." I had no idea what that sentence meant back then. I listened, but I did not understand. The words came, but they floated in the air without triggering any real processing in my brain.

Later, when I was living in my second apartment, I vividly remember that after receiving my social support payment, I did not use it to pay rent. Instead, I spent it on pleasure—on dopamine. Alcohol or anything else that excited me seemed like a better choice, as it fed my reward system.

Eventually, I fell heavily into debt, and it manifested in many harmful ways in my life. Looking back and analyzing it now, I realize that my thought process back then was structured like this: if I placed my own reward system on one side and someone else's assets on the other, my reward system would always win.

Some might interpret that as a lack of morals, even as criminal behavior. But after careful reflection, I believe it was driven by an instinct to survive. It came from deep within my subconscious. I was not consciously thinking that way, even if others might have seen it differently.

This was clearly a major bias in my internal system. I am not trying to justify it—I am simply explaining where it came from and why I behaved that way. The roots of this behavior go back to early childhood. My brain had been wired for survival, not for strategy. When in survival mode, short-term thinking takes over and long-term thinking is suppressed.

There is a saying that humans are slaves to their emotions. As mentioned earlier, in my early childhood, I began feeding my reward system with food. This behavior is often described as "eating your emotions." I was always a bit bigger than average—in terms of body fat, so to speak. My unhealthy eating habits, combined with a total lack of knowledge about nutrition, led to excess weight. This not only affected my physical health but also intensified my mental distress, deepening the cycle of body image issues and further damaging my self-esteem.

When a person feels sad, confused, or lost, the brain tries to balance emotional states with various chemicals, such as dopamine. Sugar satisfies the brain's reward system, and the feeling of a full stomach brings temporary comfort and, on some level, a sense of safety. People often find pleasure in eating—and so did I, for a long time. At the time, I did not understand that I was harming both my body and mind.

In the early stages of my life, my typical meals consisted of macaroni, minced meat, fast food, and sugary soft drinks. I also consumed far more calories than I burned. This was clearly visible in my appearance, especially since I had no underlying medical conditions to explain my weight. The root cause was trauma and an unstable emotional and reward system in my brain.

In 2005, I quit smoking cigarettes while sober. The reason at the time was a strange feeling I experienced now and then: pressure in my chest and slight difficulty breathing. I convinced myself that cigarettes were damaging my heart. As I later realized, it was likely a mild panic disorder, triggered by an unstable mind and excess caffeine. Still, quitting smoking was a good decision, even if I did it for the wrong reasons.

When I was fifteen and living on my own, one thing I clearly remember is how some of my "friends" were so nice to me at my "party center." Still, the next day, they would almost completely ignore me. I did not realize it at the time, but that kind of behavior reflects a rather selfish personality. To be fair, they were still kids back then—like I was. But we see this behavior among adults, too.

A certain amount of selfishness is necessary in life, but we also need to recognize when and how it is appropriate. For example, we must learn to say no to certain things—especially when favors only flow in one direction or when we do not have the resources to help. That is also a form of self-respect. The core principle should be to treat others as you would like to be treated. In the example I gave, I should have turned that so-called "friend" away from my door based on how they had behaved.

Social approval felt like a warm breeze in my chest and a pleasant tickling sensation in my stomach whenever other teenagers praised me. At the time, I had no idea what that feeling was.

I have had my own "tribes" throughout life. At fifteen, my tribe consisted of almost all teenagers around my age. We had some great parties, but they also caused collateral damage: broken furniture, smashed glass doors, sticky floors, and shattered lamps.

Was it worth it? That depends on how you look at it. In terms of fun—absolutely. But in terms of social cost, and my mental and physical development—definitely not.

During those days, as mentioned earlier, I dropped out of school because I had completely lost my motivation. I still remember the day I was summoned to the teacher's office at my high school. I had missed many classes and failed several exams. There were quite a few teachers present, along with the principal. They all stared at me and asked, "Jani, what are you going to do with your life?" I remember vomiting and then answering, "I don't know, but I'm quitting this high school now." It was a snap decision.

Before dropping out, I often felt uncomfortable, lost, and scared as I walked the school hallways. What had changed since upper elementary school, which was located right next door? I was living on my own. Freedom came with a sense of uncertainty, and I lacked emotional safety—though the reasons were different from before. At the time, hanging out with friends and throwing parties occasionally brought some relief.

At the age of eighteen, I enrolled in a computer course, aiming to earn an IT qualification. I attended a few classes but soon dropped out. I did not feel comfortable with the people in my class, even though they were nice. Despite my love for computers, the psychological chaos inside my head turned everything upside down.

I could not concentrate properly. I even justified my drunk driving by the good feeling it gave me; it fed my ego in that moment. My life back then was shortsighted, driven by impulses and a poor attention span. I made reckless decisions and lost valuable opportunities.

When life feels unsafe, your brain flips the "survival switch." Stress floods the bloodstream with cortisol, priming muscles to fight or flee, but it also hijacks the limbic system—the ancient circuit that cares only about the next ten minutes. At the same moment, every small escape you choose—beer fizz on the tongue, friends' laughter, a line of amphetamine—sparks a dopamine burst. Dopamine's job is to stamp the behavior "repeat for relief." The more chaotic the environment (screaming adults, eviction threats, bar-fight adrenaline), the more often that stamp gets pressed—until short-term fixes start to feel like survival itself.

Meanwhile, the prefrontal cortex—the newer brain region that plans exams, budgets, or therapy sessions—goes partly offline. Sleep loss, stimulants, and alcohol shrink its glucose supply, so long-range thinking literally runs out of fuel. Memory consolidation falters as REM cycles are sliced up; lessons from yesterday's hangover never make it into long-term storage. The result is a cognitive funnel: hundreds of future possibilities squeeze into one urgent command—relieve the pressure now.

In July 1999, I woke up on the terrace of my apartment, which was on the ground floor. The air temperature was +30 degrees Celsius, and the sun was burning my forehead. I felt miserable. I had a heavy hangover and no idea how I had ended up there. I had experienced a total blackout.

My apartment looked like a hurricane had hit it: shattered glass, food scattered across the floor, chairs knocked over. I stood there thinking, *What the hell happened?* I went to look at myself in the mirror. Physically, I seemed fine—but inside, I felt depressed and anxious.

Suddenly, there was a knock at the door. It was my neighbor who looked concerned. He told me that during the night, he had seen two people carry me into my apartment and then leave. After that, he heard the sound of things breaking inside—and then, silence.

Apparently, I had been in a fight—with myself and the furniture. For the record, my "second personality," the one that often surfaced when I drank, was named Johannes. So Johannes must have been in a bad mood that night—mostly with himself.

After the neighbor left, I collapsed to the floor. The overwhelming feeling was shame. I started talking to myself, asking: What am I doing? Who brought me home? Where had I been?

I remembered leaving the army and starting to drink while waiting for the train. I remembered boarding the train and the taste of cold beer in my mouth. But I had no memory of arriving at my hometown's train station. Eventually, I found out I had been lying outside the Shell station, unable to walk, completely drunk. Two of my friends had found me and brought me home. That is where I woke up.

Did any of this behavior make sense? No. Not at all.

The ICU lights never dim. A fluorescent halo hummed above my bed, washing the clock, the curtain, and the lone visitor's chair in the same bone-white glare. I counted sixty-three heart-monitor beeps, waiting for a familiar face to slide the curtain aside—mother, brother, even one of the party regulars eager for war stories. My family did not arrive, but some friends did.

On beep sixty-four, a nurse adjusted the IV. "Family on the way?" she asked, almost kindly.

"Soon," I lied. She smiled, noted "patient stable" on the chart, and drifted off.

Stable. The word stung harder than the chest incision. I had survived a nightclub brawl, a botched first surgery, and a liter and a half of vomit in my lungs. Yet, the only witness to that miracle was a machine that would stop beeping the moment I unplugged it. Survival, it turned out, was a solo sport.

Around beep one hundred, the thought finally landed: No rules, no safety net, no applause—just me. The adrenaline that once felt like fuel curdled into something colder. If nobody shows up when you almost die, who is going to steer you while you are alive?

I stared at the empty chair until the beeps blurred into one long tone in my mind—a monotonous question: "What happens to a survivor with no mentors to show him what surviving is for?"

The answer begins in the next chapter.

If I Were to Talk to My Younger Self

Freedom Without Structure Is a Vacuum

The moment the door closed, all external control disappeared—and with it, any sense of safety. Emptiness came faster than excitement.

Early Trauma Wires the Brain for Survival, Not Planning

Growing up in chaos trained your limbic system to chase quick dopamine hits—beer, food, applause—while the prefrontal "strategist" stayed idle in the background.

Survival Mode Hijacks Money Decisions

Rent and bills will not carry the same emotional weight as the instant buzz of alcohol or other rewards. That is why debt piles up and landlords turn hostile.

Comfort Eating Becomes Self-Sabotage

Comfort eating will start as self-soothing and end as self-sabotage. Sugar-heavy convenience food will quiet distress for a moment, then magnify body-image shame and low self-esteem, locking you in a painful cycle.

Social Approval Bought with Access Is Brittle

Party "friends" will disappear as soon as the beer runs dry. The praise might feel good in the moment, but it will not build you a real support network.

Isolation Masquerades as Independence

Living alone will feel adult—until the first crisis exposes the truth: you have no safety net and no mentors to help you recover.

Short-Term Fixes Create Long-Term Costs

Debt, weight gain, surgical complications, poor focus, and broken trust will all compound while you keep chasing temporary relief.

Shame Can Be a Catalyst or a Cage

Blackouts, wrecked apartments, ICU alarms—each of those moments will sting enough to make you question your path. But without guidance, shame will fade, and survival mode will take over again.

The Absence of Mentors Magnifies Mistakes

Here is the harshest truth: the absence of mentors will magnify mistakes. No adult will step in to help you turn experiences into lessons. You will repeat the same errors until your own body forces the reckoning—a torn chest muscle, an ICU stay.

CHAPTER 3

No Mentors, No Models

How Isolation Shapes Self-Reliance

I felt something strange in my mouth and decided to remove it. Suddenly, I woke up to nurses telling me, "Jani, you removed your ventilator tubing! We have to check that you did not hurt yourself."

I could hear the heart monitor beeping and feel the antiseptic sting in my nostrils. My bandaged chest rose and fell shallowly, each breath was a reminder of the tear. Later, I was transferred to a regular ward. A nurse glanced at the empty visitor's chair and asked, "Is any family or anyone coming to visit?"

I replied, "No, they're busy."

The truth was, I was not even sure if they knew. By that point, I had already been isolated from my family and relatives for a long time.

In that moment, I suddenly remembered those nights at fifteen, alone in my first apartment, wondering how I could fix my Nintendo controller—maybe with a paper clip. I tried using a paper clip because I had no adults around to show me how to do it properly. I felt a sense of pride and was determined not to ask for help, but deep down, I was also sad and confused.

The inner voice in my head whispered, this is what pure survival buys you—an ICU bed and no one to sign the discharge papers.

I had survived—but I was alone.

Isolation, both physical and psychological, means being separated from meaningful social contact or emotional connection. Physical isolation is being alone in a literal sense, while psychological isolation is feeling emotionally disconnected, even in the presence of others.

Though often painful, isolation can forge strong DIY (do-it-yourself) skills, as individuals learn to solve problems independently, without guidance or support. However, it also brings hidden liabilities. These may include difficulty trusting others, an inability to ask for help, emotional detachment, and long-term mental health challenges. In short, isolation can build resilience and self-reliance, but often at the expense of emotional well-being and connection—creating a survival mindset rather than one based on support, growth, or cooperation.

I have always been a relatively fast problem solver, and as I mentioned earlier, the roots of that ability likely lie in a survival mindset. This trait has manifested in many ways throughout my life. For example, when I worked in a computer shop, I once postponed a computer repair until I suddenly realized the deadline was the next morning. I stayed up the entire night working on it, practically rebuilding the entire machine—but I got it done. Asking for help was not an option, at least not in my mind.

Another example was when I was evicted from my second home in Parkano. I had not taken the eviction notice seriously, and one day, they carried my belongings out and changed the locks. After that, I kicked into action. Within about eight hours, I had moved my things into a warehouse, and within twenty-four hours, I had secured a new apartment to move them into.

There were also times when I did not know what I was going to eat the next day—not because of too many options, but because of a lack of money and stable income. In situations like that, quick problem-solving is not optional—it is about meeting basic survival needs, like food.

Looking back, it is fair to say I was hyper-independent. That trait had its advantages, but also clear downsides. As I wrote earlier, I am a quick problem solver—a skill shaped by isolation and survival. The downside, however, was that I often found myself in crises that required quick solutions. In a way, I was a crisis magnifier.

But when you consider my story, is that surprising? Not at all. Isolation shaped how I think. Since I was not part of any particular group, I did not absorb others' ways of thinking. I have always thought independently—and I still do. That independence has become one of my superpowers, though it has also brought its share of challenges.

Alongside my problem-solving skills, I have always been quite creative. In hindsight, one unfortunate downside was that this creativity became a key tool I used to commit crimes. While I was operating in survival mode—which is not a justification, but rather an explanation—it does not excuse my actions.

The day I forged a medical certificate using a printer and got caught was a major "brain fart." Still, it required creativity to pull off. Compared to my earlier talent for PC-building, it is clear that a person can also misuse their abilities and waste their potential.

Once, a person who had my money in his company's bank account was arrested. To recover the funds, I altered some invoices by inserting a different bank account number and personally took them to the bank. The goal was to get the money into our own account before it was too late—and I succeeded. However, I received jail time for this, and I knew that was likely the moment I walked into the bank. Still, I needed the money, and the urgency overrode my awareness of potential punishment.

There were many situations where I applied this skill set. You could call it "MacGyver creativity." Real creativity requires thinking outside the box—assembling a puzzle without even knowing what the pieces are. Sometimes, those pieces have to be invented. That is something I have always been good at—and still am. These days, however, my creativity serves a deeper purpose and is applied to practical and productive goals.

The survival mindset, rooted in isolation, enhanced this skill. I did not brainstorm these ideas with anyone—I was a solo operator. Over time, I have learned that I can fuel my creativity in many ways: listening to music, meditating, and drawing mind maps, for example. Perhaps even the computer and role-playing games I enjoyed in my early years played a part in developing both my problem-solving and creative thinking skills—both were essential when playing those games.

When social mammals—humans included—grow up with shaky attachment, the brain quietly rewrites its operating code. Repeated loneliness elevates baseline cortisol, the stress hormone that whispers, "Handle it yourself or perish." High cortisol enlarges and sensitizes the amygdala, the almond-shaped alarm center that scans the room for threat. An oversized amygdala is great for spotting danger but terrible for long-range planning; it yanks energy away from the prefrontal cortex, the region that budgets, studies, and resists impulse.

At the same time, oxytocin—the "safety in numbers" neuropeptide—pulses less often because hugs, praise, and dependable guidance are scarce. With fewer oxytocin washes, the brain struggles to label people as resources; it labels them as variables to manage. Result: hyper-independent circuits get over-practiced while collaboration circuits lie idle.

Put simply, chronic isolation turns the mind into a Swiss Army knife built for emergencies: quick to improvise, quick to shut down emotions that might slow a reaction, and slow to trust any solution that is not immediately at hand. Great for crisis triage; disastrous for building a life plan.

I remember one particular night in prison less for what I felt than for what I did not. The cell door clanged shut at 21:02, metal on metal, and the sound ought to have rattled my bones. Instead, it landed somewhere outside my skin, like distant fireworks you see through double-glazed windows.

My bunkmate, a thin kid with tattoos still scabbing over, sat on the lower bed and shook. He tried to hide it, but often a stifled sob slipped out and bounced off the concrete. I registered the noise, filed it as irrelevant, and went back to inventorying the room: one steel toilet, two gray blankets, three rivets missing from the desk bracket.

I lay down on the top bunk, laced my fingers behind my head, and stared at the ceiling's hairline cracks. A thought drifted past–You should say something comforting–then vanished like breath on cold glass. Comfort required warmth; I had packed none. What I had was a switch, refined over years of family fights and blackout hangovers, that could mute inconvenient feelings within seconds. I flicked it now, and the world dulled to a hum.

Somewhere below, the kid whispered a prayer. I counted heart-beats–mine stayed steady, fifty per minute. Pride flickered: look how calm you are. Then another voice–quieter, older–wondered what kind of thirty-two-year-old measures success by how little he can feel. I rolled onto my side and pressed that voice into the mattress until it stopped twitching.

In isolation, numbness becomes adaptive–like a frozen lake that holds firm underfoot. Yet emotional anesthesia, though it can be a survival skill, carries its own side effects. You cannot amputate fear without nicking joy, nor mute grief without silencing hope. The cortisone surge may spare you the panic of the moment, yet it also steals the signal that says change something. Lying there under prison fluorescents, I mistook absence of pain for strength and called the bargain even, never noticing the bill still accumulating, out of sight.

I remember it like it was yesterday–a night working as a door attendant in Helsinki. I was constantly observing the environment, scanning for possible hostile situations. I felt like an outsider and was convinced something was going to happen, even though it rarely did.

This hypervigilance stemmed from my childhood environment. When triggered, my brain would switch into freeze, fight, or flight mode. Adrenaline would start to flow—often without any immediate reason. The brain is truly fascinating.

While watching the crowd, I would absorb their energy and quickly sense trouble, doing my best to defuse it. At that point in my life, my charisma was driven by adrenaline, not empathy. In one instance, during the removal of a patron, I slammed his head against a brick wall—an act driven by instinct, not compassion. Thankfully, no serious harm occurred. These moments reflect how survival wiring can override emotional connection.

The described behavior reflects hypervigilance and a trauma-related stress response rooted in early life experiences. When a person grows up in an unpredictable or unsafe environment, the brain may become conditioned to expect danger, triggering the fight, flight, or freeze response even in relatively safe situations. This results in chronic adrenaline release, emotional numbing, and impulsive reactions. Over time, survival instincts may override empathy, leading to aggressive or defensive behavior. The individual becomes skilled at reading threats but struggles with emotional regulation, as the nervous system remains in a heightened state of alert—a hallmark of complex trauma or PTSD.

Isolation trained me to become a one-man survival toolkit. When eviction notices landed on the doormat, I could hustle day jobs, borrow a van, and relocate quickly after the locks changed. The same ingenuity that let me resurrect obsolete computers from scrap parts later produced a forged medical certificate on a battered inkjet printer. Nightclubs hired me because I could read a hostile crowd in seconds and defuse fights with the right mix of size and quick talk. I even quit cigarettes without a program, patched my own résumé, cooked on pennies, and on one night in prison, fell asleep while a bunkmate sobbed beneath me—proof that fear rarely hijacked my mission.

Yet visible victory hid a growing ledger of debt. Drunk driving fines, forged document charges, and court fees stacked up faster than my day-wage cash. A torn chest muscle and an ICU stay revealed the bodily price of adrenaline bravado, while evictions and late-rent threats exposed the financial chaos beneath the hustle. Party companions disappeared the moment the beer or bail money ran out, leaving friendships charred at the edges. Alcohol, amphetamine, and steroids eroded my liver, sleep, and sanity; psychotic episodes and chronic shame seeped into the quiet hours. Three times the system claimed years of my life in prison—interest payments on a loan of unchecked independence.

It was a spring morning in 2014. I stood in the yard of Tampere University Hospital. A warm wind blew across my face, but I did not feel anything—emotionally numb, despite being released from the hospital.

The night before, I had taken a taxi there because my heart had suddenly started racing, and I could barely walk. I was alone at home.

I arrived, and my heart rate was around two hundred. The doctors told me I had arrhythmia. One of them said, "This will be over in a second—we will give you some medicine. It will not feel pleasant, but it will bring your heart rhythm back to normal."

I will never forget the sensation. As they administered the medicine—three times—it felt like a crushing weight on my chest. I was certain I was about to "throw my spoon in the corner," so to speak, and cross into another dimension. But I thought, So what? Bring it on.

When the medication did not work, they gave me a sedative through an IV, and I fell asleep. Thankfully, I woke up the next morning.

Back then, it was my skills that kept me afloat—but emotionally, I remained anchored in place, somewhere deep in childhood. I had frozen myself.

Psychologically, this kind of detachment—emotional numbing—is a classic response to chronic stress and trauma. In my case, it had been cultivated over years of survival-mode living. Growing up in emotionally unstable and unsupported environments, I had trained myself not to feel. When a child does not feel safe, the mind develops defense mechanisms: it disconnects from emotional pain to avoid being overwhelmed. But the same shield that protects also isolates.

If I Were to Talk to My Younger Self

Survival Skills Are Not a Life Plan

You will build your life around survival—hyper-independence, emotional numbing, and crisis-driven thinking. Yes, you will become skilled at quick problem-solving, resourcefulness, and creativity, but remember: these skills are born of necessity, not true planning. Survival mode can save you, but it cannot guide you.

Living Alone Feels Like Strength but Blocks Growth

Living alone in your head and your world will feel like strength. You will grow self-reliant and distrustful, but that same detachment will block long-term growth and meaningful relationships. Asking for help is not a weakness—it is wisdom.

Shutting Down Emotions Delays Healing

To protect yourself, you'll shut down joy, grief, and empathy. It will make you seem cold—even during significant moments like ICU stays, prison, or family events. But that numbness will not protect you forever; it only delays healing.

Intelligence Without Patience Becomes Recklessness

Your intelligence will flare under pressure. Sometimes, you will channel it into reckless or even illegal shortcuts, such as forging documents or gaming systems. Later, you will learn that the same creativity, if harnessed with patience, can build your future instead of breaking it.

Instability Rewires the Brain—But Wiring Can Change

Years of instability will make your amygdala overactive, always scanning for danger, while trust and connection chemistry (oxytocin) runs low. You will be built for emergencies but unprepared for a calm, steady life. Do not blame yourself—it is wiring, not weakness. Wiring can be reshaped.

Detachment Is Not Toughness

You will confuse emotional detachment with toughness—thinking that not reacting in prison or staying stone-faced in a hospital bed is control. It is not; It is suppression. Real strength is feeling pain and facing it without running away.

Independence Alone Will Break You

You will believe you can carry it all alone. On the outside, you will look like you can. But inside, the weight will show up as health breakdowns, legal trouble, broken connections, and shame. Independence matters, but interdependence saves.

The Emotional Toll of Going It Alone

In 2014, after I was released from the hospital, I visited the hospital café. There, I ran into someone I had known from my early days in Parkano. He asked what had happened, and I briefly explained. He smiled and said, "I can see your life's not going so well," then walked away.

I did not feel anything in particular after his comment. I bought a cup of coffee and stepped outside.

Standing in the hospital yard, I began to think about what he had said. Maybe that was his way of communicating—or perhaps, deep down, he was somehow pleased about my situation. I felt a weight in my chest. Although I was not consciously analyzing what had happened in the café, my mind and body were clearly responding to something.

At that time in my life, I did not worry about whether I would live or die. That kind of indifference was not a healthy way to think about oneself. Maybe that sudden, unexpected encounter—his face, his words—triggered something in me. Perhaps my mind and body were trying to send a message—something deeper than the fact that I had experienced atrial fibrillation.

I remember one sunny, warm summer day in 2005. I was sitting in my car after finishing a workout at the gym. I felt confident and energetic. As I enjoyed the rush of positive thoughts, I decided to call an acquaintance. He answered, and we agreed to meet later—maybe for a few drinks.

I knew I had problems with alcohol, or more specifically, with my behavior while drinking. But I felt so good after the workout that I told myself, What the hell—I can control it this time.

As we started drinking, we eventually decided to head to Tampere, a larger city about eighty kilometers south. In hindsight, this was a bad idea. We kept drinking, and I started to get drunk. I told myself, if I can handle ten beers, I can handle twenty. I convinced myself everything would go smoothly—no harm done.

The evening continued, and the warning signs appeared. I got heavily drunk and suddenly realized I was in a bar located in the same building as the train station where we had arrived. The last things I remember were a platter full of shots and a bouncer dragging me out. Apparently, I had started to misbehave again.

Before I opened my eyes, I listened to the silence around me. Then came the smell—concrete and dust. I opened my eyes and realized I was lying half under someone's car in a parking garage, without shoes or a phone. It was partly hilarious. Luckily, I still had my wallet—not that it had much in it.

I walked out and saw the bar next door. I needed shoes, so I went into a nearby secondhand shop. The cashier looked both amused and scared as I walked in barefoot and announced, "I need shoes." I bought some funny-looking winter boots with my last five euros—in the middle of summer.

At the train station, by coincidence, I ran into another acquaintance. He took me to his place and lent me money for a train ticket home.

It was a textbook example of chasing short-term rewards. Survival loves applause; strategy loves preparation. That night, I chose applause, but reality hit hard when I woke up in that parking garage. No plans, no goals—another cheap dopamine fix.

Between 2000 and 2016, it felt like everything was constantly on my radar. I was always scanning the environment, hyperaware of movement and sound. I often had the feeling that people were staring at me or laughing behind my back. A stranger's smile or a glance in a grocery store could trigger a flood of paranoia.

Every time the phone rang—especially from an unknown number— or if I heard someone walking in the stairwell, my body would tense up. My attention was always focused on potential threats. I ground my teeth at night without realizing it—a fact discovered later by a dentist. My jaw was always tight, and I sometimes felt pressure in my chest while awake.

When I was discharged from the mental hospital in 2014, I vividly remember standing outside the Lidl store near my home. I felt an invisible force—almost like an aura—trying to stop me from entering. The anxiety was overwhelming, as if everyone inside were staring and whispering, "Do not come in." I closed my eyes for a second, took a breath, and forced myself through the door.

Back then, it was normal for me to sit with my back against the wall wherever I went, always scanning exits and preparing for "what if" scenarios. My mind constantly played out worst-case outcomes, rarely allowing space for positive thoughts. Even when nothing happened–and usually nothing ever did–my nervous system stayed on high alert, wounded by imagined threats.

Chronic anxiety is not a passing feeling; it is a constant state of tension–a jaw that never unclenches, a body that never fully relaxes, and a mind always half-listening for danger that may never come. Chronic anxiety and long-term isolation are closely linked in the brain. Normally, social connection triggers the release of oxytocin–a neuropeptide that calms the nervous system, lowers cortisol, and signals safety. But in isolation, oxytocin buffering is minimal or absent. As a result, the sympathetic nervous system— responsible for the "fight or flight" response–stays idling high, even in non-threatening situations. This state, known as hypervig- ilance, keeps the brain scanning for danger, interpreting neutral stimuli (like a stranger's smile or footsteps in the stairwell) as potential threats. Over time, this rewires neural circuits to favor short-term reactivity over long-term calm. The brain becomes a survival tool–sharp in crisis but prone to exhaustion, tension, and mistrust. Without consistent social safety signals, the body forgets how to relax.

I felt a bead of sweat roll down my skin as the classroom remained completely silent. I could smell the overhead projector and feel the warm draft it produced. My body felt frozen as I tried to avoid my teacher's gaze. I was standing in front of my class in high school, during a time when my motivation was low. All eyes were on me. I was the center of everyone's attention.

My chest tightened, my stomach dropping as if the floor had tilted. Heat surged into my cheeks–a flush I could not escape. My gaze locked downward, avoiding the teacher's eyes, while sweat prickled and slid across my skin. Words jammed in my throat, each one heavier than the last. Shame–that ancient social alarm, fired to keep me in line its sting as sharp as physical pain.

I wondered why I even went to the front of the class, knowing full well I had not prepared my homework. I studied my teacher's face before walking up there, and I am quite sure she already knew. Rather than flee, I chose to fight. I stood there and said, "I think I have early dementia, but I am terribly sorry; I cannot do my presentation. I forgot what I was going to say, even though I remembered it at home."

It felt like the safest option—pretending I had done the work when I had not. Still, I punished myself in my thoughts afterward. Worse yet, my reputation dropped in my teacher's eyes.

The shame trailed me long after the classroom emptied. I avoided certain hallways, ducked out of sight when classmates gathered, and rewrote the scene in my head with sharper comebacks that never came in time. Without any model for repairing mistakes or forgiving myself, the moment calcified. Nights stretched longer, replaying the heat in my cheeks under the shower spray.

Avoidance dulled the sting briefly, but each retreat taught my brain the same lesson—hide now, and you will hurt later. Shame did not sting—it rewired me for withdrawal. Without mentors or models to show me how to recover, it became my harshest teacher, teaching avoidance over growth. Each episode pushed me further into my own corner. Shame built the walls, but I was the one who decided to live inside them.

In 2010, another friend of mine passed away when his heart failed during sleep. When I received the news, I felt as if the entire world paused for a moment. I became acutely aware of the fresh scent of the air freshener in my car. At the same time, sweat formed on my forehead and along my sides, and I felt a slight pressure in my chest. I pulled over and parked the car.

As I sat in my car, wondering why this had happened to my friend, my subconscious mind shielded me from any emotional reaction, and numbness set in. Shaped by past experiences, my mind had no toolkit for processing sorrow. My survival mechanism was simply to ignore the sadness and keep moving forward.

As the days and weeks passed, I kept exercising and, one night, went out for a few drinks. I remember a friend sitting next to me, clearly trying to do the right thing as he spoke to me about the situation. I vividly recall feeling nothing in particular—no sadness. Without realizing it at the time, I was drowning myself in activity. This was my way of surviving situations like this.

Sadness can sometimes strip away the raw survival mode, but in this—and many other cases—it didn't happen to me. Instead, it revealed where the connection was missing, with roots in my past where I had lost loved ones and accumulated other experiences described earlier. In my case, situations where I was supposed to grieve only strengthened my isolation. If shame built the walls, grief reinforced the isolation within them.

Each emotion carried its own survival script, and I played them out with the tools at hand—beer cans, white powder, steroids, or a fridge full of sugar. What looked like choice was often compulsion—a reflex trained by repetition.

Pride's crash left me empty, and beer was the shortcut back to feeling something. A can in my hand turned silence into noise, shame into laughter—for a few hours. It never lasted, but for the length of a weekend, I could pretend grandiosity had not collapsed.

Anxiety's gnawing edge pushed me toward amphetamine. Two minutes after a line, the restlessness melted into a sense of control and speed. My chest unclenched, my thoughts aligned, and I could finally breathe—or at least that is how it felt. Later came the paranoia, but by then, the loop was already set.

Shame's burn drove me inward, and steroids became my armor. Bigger muscles were supposed to silence the voice calling me weak. Each injection promised confidence, but underneath, I only layered more fragility onto an already cracked foundation.

Sadness and grief demanded comfort, and food filled the gap. Sugar dulled the edge; warm meals became temporary safety. I ate to soften the ache, never realizing that every bite also deepened my disconnection from my own body. Each fix promised relief, but none delivered healing. The spiral only tightened.

Ignoring Possible Mentors

Looking back, I see the outlines of people who could have been mentors—if only I had had the ears to hear them.

My math teacher came to the prison once a week, chalk dust still on his jacket, patience carved into his voice. He treated us not like criminals but like students, daring us to believe in formulas instead of fatalism. At the time, I nodded and solved the problems, but the deeper lesson—that discipline could rebuild a broken life—was already in my mind.

In the psych ward, one nurse paused longer than she had to when she checked my vitals. Her question—"Are you sleeping at all?"—carried a weight I ignored. She was pointing at the engine under the chaos, at the sleepless nights above all else that drove me toward psychosis. But I heard it only as routine small talk, not as the lifeline it was meant to be.

My army sergeant, back when I still wore the uniform, once said, "You're quick, Havunen, but you're always looking sideways." He was naming my restless scanning—a survival habit that never let me stay present. Instead of hearing wisdom, I laughed it off, proud of my ability to dodge authority.

They were all there—chalk, clipboard, uniform—but I was too deafened by pride, shame, and noise to let their words take root.

The door clicked shut, and for the first time at fifteen, no adult voice followed. The flat buzzed with silence—a weak bulb and the hum of an old fridge. I cracked a beer, stared out at the neon bleeding from the Shell station, and realized freedom was not the same as safety.

That empty room taught me more than any teacher. No grand-mother's breath, no stepfather's threats—just me, a chair by the window, and a question that had no answer: now what? The lone-liness pressed as heavy as the beer in my stomach.

That night, and many after it, carried the same truth I would later find in courtrooms, psychward corridors, and hospital wards: survival is not applause. An empty room, an empty chair, an empty hallway—all whispered the same refrain: if I broke, no one else was there to put me back together.

And yet, those lonely nights became strange pivots. They could have swallowed me whole. Instead, they hardened into lines pointing forward.

The next chapter is about those lines—the rock bottoms that almost broke me, and the invisible pivots that did not.

If I Were to Talk to My Younger Self

Encounters Are Mirrors

If I could talk to you now, I would remind you that encounters act as mirrors. That single comment—"your life's not going so well"—cut deeper than you admitted. Your chest tightened, your breath grew heavy. What you called indifference to life and death was not resilience at all; it was numbness.

The Trap of Short-Term Rewards

You fell into the trap of short-term rewards. Beer turned silence into noise. Amphetamines turned restlessness into speed. Steroids turned shame into armor. Sugar turned grief into comfort.

Anxiety as a Constant Companion

Anxiety became your constant background noise. You scanned exits without realizing it, clenched your jaw until your teeth ached, and carried tightness in your chest. Isolation drained you of oxytocin, keeping your nervous system on permanent alert. Even neutral glances felt threatening.

Shame, the Harsh Teacher

Shame became your harshest teacher. Classroom failures and cover-up lies taught you to withdraw. With no mentors to show you how to repair and recover, you built walls and decided to live inside them.

Grief Without Tools Becomes Numbing

Grief could have been a doorway to connection, but you didn't have the tools. Instead of mourning, you threw yourself into workouts, drinks, distractions, and endless busyness. Surviving meant numbing yourself.

Lifelines You Couldn't Yet Hear

And yes, mentors crossed your path—a teacher, a nurse, a sergeant—each one leaving clues you could not yet hear. Survival mode kept you deaf to lifelines. But they were there—proof that you were never completely alone.

CHAPTER 4

Moments That Could Have Broken Me (But Did Not)

Rock Bottoms and Invisible Pivots

It was an ordinary day in 2011, though in hindsight, nothing about that period of my life was ordinary. I was staying on a friend's couch, waiting for the day I would soon have to walk into jail. The couch was worn, brown leather, heavy with the smell of sweat and time, as if it had absorbed the restless nights of everyone who had ever collapsed on it. A single dim light hung in the room, and a small television flickered in the background—the kind of scene that captures a person's emptiness better than words ever could.

I remember ordering a family-sized pizza, a handful of chocolate bars, and a double portion of kebab. It was gluttony disguised as comfort. When I finished, my body rebelled—my heart raced, and a wave of sickness washed over me. I thought to myself, *Is this even possible? Can food alone make me feel like I am about to collapse?* But of course it can, when a man consumes several thousand empty calories in a single sitting.

My friend looked at me with a half-smile and asked, "Jani, are you trying to kill yourself on my couch?" I laughed it off, muttering something careless in return. Yet behind that laughter was the quiet truth: this was not about food but about the exhaustion of a way of living that was slowly breaking me down.

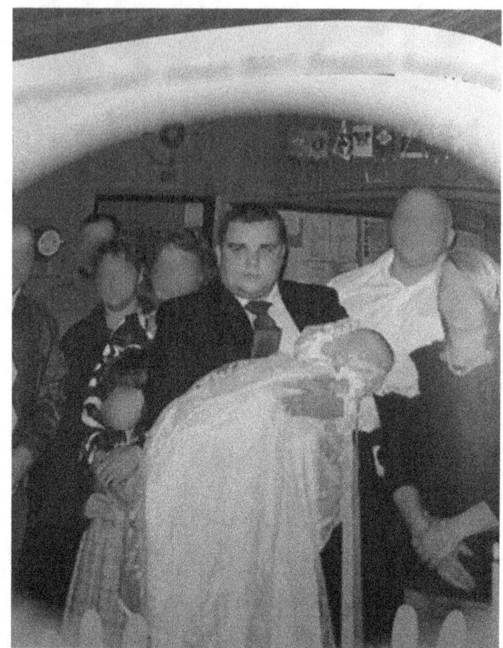

**Me weighing about 147 kg – at one of my lowest points,
physically and mentally.**

That night was not unique. It was one of many episodes where my life seemed to pause on the edge of an ending, only to continue on—not with a full stop, but with a comma. Beneath the surface stretched years of instability and, more than anything, a tangled and troubled state of mind, the kind I have mentioned before.

But for my friend's brown leather couch, that night was indeed the end. After I moved on, he had to throw it away; the stench had seeped too deeply into it. In a way, that discarded couch became a symbol of my condition—of how far I had let myself go and how much of my chaos I carried with me into the spaces of others.

My life has been marked by many rock bottoms. Some of them I have already shared earlier in this book, yet they continue to echo within me. Let us return to a few of those moments and uncover some new ones as well. In revisiting these events, I will reflect on the invisible pivots they contained—quiet turning points that only revealed their meaning long after the fall.

I moved into my own apartment at the age of fifteen, carrying with me the weight of a life that had already been far from ordinary. I was lost, frightened, and utterly unprepared to shoulder the responsibility for myself. I had no tools, no guidance, no foundation to stand on. Yet, I have come to believe that even the harshest events carry a kind of purpose. This one, too—like those that came before it—was a crossroads that could have broken me but instead became part of the map that shaped who I am.

The feeling of being an outsider has followed me since my earliest days—a constant shadow. My mind has always worked differently: I see the world as a network of invisible lines, a map of relationships and perspectives drawn between people. I cannot help but analyze—the tilt of a head, the flicker of an expression, the currents flowing between gestures, words, and silences. Even as a child, my brain was busy deciphering the subtle codes of human connection.

Living in shifting families—or perhaps it is more honest to call them communes—honed this instinct. When I moved out on my own, still a boy, it forged the skill into something sharper. As an outsider, I learned to scout the world differently, to read spaces and people as landscapes to be navigated with care. Over time, this became both a survival strategy and a hidden strength—what I now think of as an invisible pivot, a tool that allowed me to adapt, endure, and sometimes even see further than others.

But tools can cut both ways. In the darker, messier seasons of my life, this relentless awareness turned inward and became my enemy. I will explore how that played out more deeply in Chapter Five.

Convictions and Admissions

When I first walked into jail in 2005, I realized almost immediately that life behind bars was its own strange world. The air carried a different mentality, one shaped by walls and limits. Conversations buzzed with grandiose schemes—prison was a place where everyone seemed to brainstorm their next "brilliant idea," as if the bars themselves could not restrain ambition, only distort it.

My first conviction—nine months in an open prison—taught me about humiliation and the slow erosion of identity. I was no longer in charge of myself; my freedom was trimmed down to schedules and permissions. Still, that first sentence left little true wisdom behind. I noticed the patterns—in staff, inmates, and the rituals of control—and I felt the value of freedom once it was returned. Yet clearly, I had not grasped it deeply enough.

The second time, in a closed prison, the stripping away was harsher. Every door was opened for me, every movement dictated. Autonomy shrank to nothing. Looking back, I sometimes think those walls may have saved me. In that confinement, I learned about friendship, the weight of status, and how it governed the smallest gestures between men.

By 2016, during my last sentence, I was stronger—not yet free but more aware. The prison was rural and, compared to many, almost pleasant. Yet even in this "gentler" place, the effects of confinement revealed themselves. I watched men of stature—even foreign generals—shrink into childlike behaviors. Perhaps it was a coping mechanism of the brain, but it showed me how environments can bend human dignity.

These were moments that could have broken me. Instead, they imposed structure, discipline, and routine—harsh gifts that left their mark. I think of those years as rungs on a ladder: I began at the bottom, climbing step by step. Each sentence forged me further, and with every climb, I discovered invisible pivots—small turns of fate that shifted my direction away from a life that was never truly mine to live.

My short time in Ibiza felt like stepping into two different worlds. On one side, it was the dream I had seen only on movie screens: sunlit beaches, beautiful women, music pulsing through the nights, and parties that seemed to have no end. There was a thrill in the air, a current of excitement laced with danger. I remember the military police pressing through massive crowds to break up fights—their presence both frightening and surreal, as if chaos itself had become part of the spectacle. There was laughter, wild stories, and a sense of belonging—at least on the surface.

But there was another side, one far less glamorous. It was a blur of alcohol and drugs, of memories fractured and bent out of shape. I recall chasing strange visions, stumbling through the night like a child pursuing fairy-tale creatures after swallowing sleeping pills without ever intending to sleep. These were not adventures—they were confusions, distortions, signs of something breaking inside me.

Too many mornings began with the same refrain: others recounting my actions, filling in the gaps of nights I could not remember. What they told me was rarely flattering and often shameful. Yet I still refused to listen. The lessons were there, circling me like vultures, but I turned away.

In Ibiza, one friend finally told us he would never spend another moment in our company. His words should have been enough. There were other signs too—waking beneath a car in a strange city, shouting senseless things at someone I cared about, watching bridges smolder before they even had a chance to burn. Each moment was a warning, but I ignored it.

Looking back, I see them now for what they were: invisible pivots, subtle turning points quietly insisting, "This life is not for you. Stop before it swallows you whole."

After the surgery in 2007, I woke in the intensive care unit, surrounded by machines and fluorescent light. But I did not truly wake in the way one should—with the clarity that life is fragile, that it can be cut short without warning. It should have been my moment of reckoning, but it was not. Instead, my thoughts drifted only briefly to the distance between myself and my family, to the quiet isolation I had built around me. Then, as quickly as it came, the reflection faded.

Seven years later, in 2014, I found myself in a hospital again, this time with a heart condition. Once more, the lesson slipped past me. I was drained, wandering through life without direction, unable to care whether I lived or died. It was not strength that kept me alive, but indifference. I recall standing in the hospital yard when an acquaintance crossed my path. His comment about the state of my life struck somewhere deep—a flicker of recognition—yet I still refused to see what it meant.

And yet, something stirred beneath the fog. Not in bold declarations, or lightning epiphanies, but quietly—in the deep chambers of the subconscious. These moments, though they looked like endings, began to forge a whisper of truth: I was walking the wrong road.

I see now that they were rock bottoms—but not only that. Each was an invisible pivot, nudging me step by hesitant step toward another path. They did not save me in an instant, but they began to reshape the scaffolding of my mind, dripping slowly into the bucket that would one day overflow and form new values. Still, I know how easily they could have been the final chapters. More than once, my story came close to ending there, in those sterile hospital rooms.

In the mental hospital in 2014, I came to a strange realization: compared to many of the patients around me, I was, in fact, quite healthy. The thought struck me with an odd mixture of relief and discomfort. I will explore more deeply, in Chapter Five, what my mind was like in those days of psychosis. But what mattered most was this—I could have collapsed completely then. I did not. Even in the midst of shadows and confusion, something in me held.

Looking back, I know that I often sensed, deep inside, that my way of living made no sense. Yet I pushed forward, as if momentum itself carried me. I told myself I lacked the will to stand alone, and perhaps at the time I believed it.

In the courtrooms, I carried nicknames—"Tinkerer," "Balloon"— born of my own actions and appearance. Back then, they stirred no reflection. I laughed with others, treating them as jokes, and even taking a strange pride in the notoriety. Only later, when I revisited those memories, did the sting of shame and humiliation surface. Those names revealed the loss of respect I had allowed to define me. They should have been warning lights, pivots pointing me toward self-awareness, toward change.

There are always two sides to the coin. My exhausting lifestyle and the crooked way of thinking that came with it dragged me into trouble time and again, but they also hardened something in me—resilience, born out of necessity. I relied mostly on myself. Yes, at times people offered help, but the weight of survival rested squarely on my own shoulders.

The truth is, I experienced many rock bottoms. Yet each one carried within it another side—an invisible pivot, a fragile but steady place to lean against. These hidden turns did not lift me out all at once, but they marked the slow shaping of a life that, against the odds, refused to end where it might have.

Looking back, I often wonder why certain rock bottoms did not break me, even when they easily could have. At the time, I did not interpret them as warnings. I laughed at nicknames that should have filled me with shame, ignored signals from my collapsing health, and brushed aside the silent voice telling me that my path was unsustainable. Only much later did I begin to see these experiences as pivots that reshaped me from the inside out.

Neuroscience offers an explanation for this delayed recognition. The brain is not a static machine; it is constantly rewiring itself through a process called neuroplasticity. Experiences—whether traumatic, humiliating, or redemptive—leave imprints on the brain's networks. At the time, those imprints may not feel like lessons, but over time, the repeated exposure to stress, failure, or shame can change how the brain processes reality.

Resilience, too, has a neurological basis. Under prolonged stress, the brain releases cortisol, which, in high doses, can impair memory and decision-making. Yet the brain also builds coping circuits in response. Some people collapse under stress; others adapt, drawing strength from hardships that once threatened them. Psychologists often call this post-traumatic growth—the phenomenon in which individuals not only survive adversity but eventually transform it into a foundation for new meaning.

When I think about my time in hospitals or courtrooms, I can now see how my brain was slowly reframing those events, even when I consciously refused to acknowledge them. The moments of shame, the loss of autonomy, even the humor I used as a shield—they were all signals that my mind was gathering, waiting for the right time to be understood.

In hindsight, the pivots were not sudden revelations but gradual rewrites of my mental wiring. Neuroscience suggests that healing often happens this way—not through one dramatic awakening, but through countless small adjustments that eventually shift the course of a life.

If I Were Talking to My Younger Self

Rock Bottoms Are Not Endings

If I could speak to you, I would tell you that rock bottoms do not have to be endings. I know the hospital stays, the prison walls, and the blurred nights in Ibiza all felt like they could be the full stop of your story, but they were not. They became commas instead—pauses that made space for change, even if you could not see it then.

Survival Still Counts

Survival is messy, but it still counts. The beer, the steroids, the reckless nights, the heavy meals—they were flawed ways of numbing pain, yes, but they were also proof that you refused to give up completely. Even in your clumsiest coping, there was a stubborn will to endure. That matters.

Being an Outsider Was Preparation

I would tell you, too, that feeling like an outsider was not the curse you thought it was. All that scanning of people's gestures, words, and moods—the hyperawareness that left you exhausted—was also forging sensitivity and insight. One day, that same skill could guide you instead of tormenting you.

Discipline Was Hiding in Harsh Places

Even in the harshest places, discipline was hiding. Prisons gave you routines, repetitions, and small wins. They were cruel gifts, but still gifts. If I could whisper it to you, I would say: do not ignore those lessons. Structure, even when imposed, can become scaffolding for something stronger.

The Signals Were Always There

The signals were always there. The nicknames in courtrooms, friends quietly drifting away, the pounding heart after a binge— each one was a warning light. You laughed them off and dismissed them, but they were whispers of truth: this path is not for you.

Change Is Slow, But Possible

And finally, I would tell you that change is slow but possible. The brain rewires itself little by little. Healing rarely arrives in a flash of revelation. It comes through countless small pivots, through scars that become lessons. Be patient.

Why I Kept Moving Forward Anyway

If survival was so draining, why didn't I stop?

It is a question I have asked myself many times. On the surface, the answer seems obvious: when life becomes unbearable, one either collapses or changes course. Yet my reality was different. I often stood on the edge of collapse—exhausted, humiliated, and without the strength to carry myself forward—yet I still stumbled on.

There were two roads before me. One was to give up entirely— to let myself break under the weight of exhaustion, substances, shame, and the countless rock bottoms that pressed in on me. That road was tempting because it promised an end to the struggle. Many times I thought I had reached the point where surrender was inevitable.

But instead of collapsing, I somehow kept moving. Not gracefully, not with purpose, but in a half-blind, half-stubborn shuffle forward. I carried no clear vision, no grand plan. Often, I did not even care whether I lived or died. Yet something—resilience, instinct, or perhaps sheer inertia—pushed me to keep going.

This paradox has haunted me: why persist in a life I barely valued? Only later did I begin to see that even in the blur of survival, invisible pivots were forming. Each humiliation, each hospital visit, each moment of shame quietly carved out space for a different path. I could not see it then, but stumbling forward became, in its own way, the first step toward change.

If sheer exhaustion and self-destruction had been the only ingredients in my life, collapse would have been inevitable. And yet, I did not collapse—not fully. Something, or rather a set of things, kept nudging me forward when the easier option would have been to give up entirely. Looking back, I can see the small, hidden drivers that held me up, often without my awareness. They were neither heroic nor particularly rational.

Even when everything else crumbled—health, relationships, reputation—pride refused to leave me. It was not the noble kind of pride that lifts a man toward betterment, but the raw, distorted kind that refuses defeat. It whispered, you will not be the one who breaks here, not now, not like this.

Pride can destroy, but paradoxically, it can also preserve. Mine worked like a pilot flame in the darkness. I refused to be seen as the one who completely collapsed. Even when shame weighed heavily, some stubborn instinct told me to keep moving, even if I had no clear direction.

That pride was not pretty, and at times it chained me to foolish choices, but in hindsight, it also served as disguised resilience. It would not let me go under.

In the chaos of bigger defeats, I found energy in small victories. In prison, the act of exercising—lifting weights, walking laps, feeling the body strengthen—gave me something tangible. Each repetition was a reminder that I still had agency over at least one part of myself.

Fixing a broken piece of technology, solving a problem with my hands, even something as mundane as quitting cigarettes—all these micro-victories mattered. They were like breadcrumbs scattered along a path I could not yet see clearly. Each one whispered: You are still capable of change, of mastery, of discipline, however small.

I did not always celebrate them at the time, but in retrospect, they were vital. Without those wins, no matter how minor, the weight of the losses would have suffocated me completely. No man survives alone, though for much of my life I tried. Relationships were fragile, often strained, yet they carried me further than I realized.

Meeting Riina became one of the anchors of my existence. Her presence reminded me that connection was still possible, that I could be more than the chaos I had carried for years. With her, I glimpsed the possibility of a different kind of life—steadier, kinder, and more whole.

With Riina came others who anchored me in their own ways. One of them was Mr. Damien, the Rottweiler who became my companion. Animals have no interest in your reputation, your failures, or the nicknames you acquire in a courtroom. To him, I was simply his person. That unconditional loyalty steadied me in a way words cannot fully capture.

These bonds—whether human or canine—reminded me that I was not completely lost to the world. Even when I felt unworthy of others, their presence told me otherwise. They were living pivots—proof that I still had reasons to remain standing.

Echoes of Survival

Sometimes the things that keep us alive are not immediate revelations but echoes that return much later. Words, once spoken, can sit dormant for years before taking root.

I still remember blunt lines from friends, the quiet patience of a teacher, and the critique of a sergeant. At the time, I often dismissed them, laughed them off, or felt humiliated by them. But their voices remained in the background, waiting. Years later, in quieter moments, those words surfaced and forced me to reckon with them.

The human brain works this way—feedback does not always yield instant change. Often, it lingers, embedding itself into the subconscious, shaping the way we process life without us even noticing. Only later did I realize those seeds had been planted. And when the ground of my life finally softened enough, they began to grow.

The most mysterious driver of all was the faint image of a different me—a future Jani who lived another kind of life. The vision was never clear, never detailed, but it was there. Sometimes, it appeared in fleeting moments—a thought while watching someone live with dignity, or a picture of myself free from the fog of substances and shame.

I could not hold that image for long. It slipped away quickly, drowned out by the noise of my life. But even its faint presence mattered. It gave me a compass—however shaky—pointing somewhere beyond my current destruction.

That vision was not of wealth or glory. It was simpler: a version of me who could stand straight, live without constant fear or chaos, and walk into a room without feeling like an outsider trapped in his own skin.

And though I could not reach him then, that imagined self kept me moving forward, stumbling as I was. It told me that collapse was not the only option—that survival might one day turn into living.

None of these drivers on their own would have been enough. Pride without small wins would have curdled into arrogance. Small wins without relationships would have felt hollow.

Relationships without echoes of feedback would have been taken for granted. And glimpses of a future self without any anchor would have vanished like smoke. But together, these fragments created a fragile scaffolding that held me up. They carried me across the years when logic alone would have led me to collapse.

Survival, in the end, was not a single act of strength but the accumulation of these subtle drivers. They were not glorious, but they were enough. "Enough" was all I needed to keep stumbling forward until I could finally begin to walk with purpose.

Resilience is often described as strength, but in my experience, it felt more like scar tissue—thickened layers built from repeated wounds. Emotional scar tissue does not grow cleanly or beautifully; it hardens in awkward shapes, sometimes limiting movement, but it also protects. Each hospital stay, each courtroom humiliation, each night of blurred memory added another layer. While much of it was maladaptive, it was still resilience.

Even the coping mechanisms that damaged me—the beer I drank to dull the noise of the world, the steroids I used to feel stronger, the substances I leaned on to numb reality—contained, in their own distorted way, a determination to survive discomfort. I was not surrendering to pain but wrestling with it in the only ways I knew. They were poor tools, yes, but tools nonetheless—proof that some part of me refused to give up.

The brain itself adapts in this way. Neuroscience shows that repeated patterns of survival carve grooves in our neural networks. Each time I endured—through brute pride, numbing substances, or sheer stubbornness—those experiences etched themselves deeper. The brain, like a well-worn path, began to assume that moving forward, however chaotically, was the only option.

This explains why I often kept going without any strategy, without even caring whether I lived or died. The grooves were already there, pushing me forward almost by default. Collapse might have been easier, but my mind had already been wired to stumble forward—to repeat survival even when it seemed meaningless.

In hindsight, I see that this scaffolding was both a curse and a gift. It kept me alive when reason alone might not have. It was far from graceful—tangled with substances, mistakes, and shame—but it was enough. Emotional scar tissue, coupled with the brain's wiring, built a rough framework that held me upright until I could build something stronger.

The truth is simple: my forward motion was not noble—it was necessity. I was not marching toward a vision; I was stumbling away from collapse. Yet even blind necessity has value. It kept me moving long enough to collect fragments—a teacher's patience, a nurse's question, a partner's love—that later formed a foundation. Rock bottoms showed me what survival looked like.

But here is the catch: while the outside story unfolded with fights, courts, bars, and prison gates, the real battlefield was inside. The scars of earlier losses—like my uncle's death—still echoed through every relationship, shaping how much I trusted and how quickly I withdrew. The peer groups that praised me when the beer flowed but vanished the morning after left me hollow, confirming the old suspicion that I was an outsider to be used. Thrill-seeking blurred into emptiness, and applause into shame. Even solitude, which once tasted like freedom, began to feel like exposure—a reminder that the fantasy of independence was cracking.

That is where the next chapter begins: not in the chaos of events, but in the fallout of emotions they left behind.

If I Could Speak to My Younger Self

Pride Can Both Chain and Carry You

Even distorted pride has power. It stopped me from collapsing completely, even when shame and exhaustion pressed in. I would tell you that pride is not always noble, but it can be fuel—do not let it blind you.

Small Wins Matter More Than You Think

Lifting weights in prison, fixing broken tech, or quitting cigarettes might have felt trivial, but each one was a reminder: you are not powerless. I would tell you to honor those crumbs of progress—they are survival disguised as discipline.

Connections Are Anchors

From Riina's presence to the loyalty of Damien and Pulla, relationships carried me further than substances ever did. I would tell you to trust those bonds—they are lifelines, even when you feel unworthy of them.

Feedback Does Not Disappear

The words of friends, teachers, or even a blunt sergeant do not always change you in the moment, but they linger. They sink into the subconscious and resurface when the soil is ready. I would tell you not to laugh them off so quickly.

Future Visions Matter—Even Faint Ones

Those fleeting glimpses of a different Jani—standing tall, free of chaos, no longer an outsider—were not fantasies. They were your compass. However blurred, they kept you stumbling in the right direction.

Resilience Is Scarring Tissue

Beer, steroids, substances—even maladaptive coping showed one thing: you refused to give up. It was messy, it was ugly, but it was survival. Scar tissue does not look pretty, but it holds you together until you can heal.

Survival Is Not Glorious—but It Is Enough

You were not walking toward a vision. You were stumbling away from collapse. And still, that was enough. Those stumbles gave you time to gather fragments—patience, loyalty, discipline—that later built the scaffolding of a new life.

CHAPTER 5

Emotional Fallout

Ghosts That Stayed

I was twelve when my uncle died. But before anyone in my family knew, before any phone call or whisper reached our home, I dreamt of white horses.

That night, they came rushing across an endless field—luminous, weightless, their hooves not striking the earth but gliding as if through air itself. I watched them run, untethered, free yet unreachable, carrying with them something I could not name. When I woke, I felt unsettled. I did not know why—only that the dream had carved itself into me with unusual sharpness, refusing to fade like ordinary dreams.

The next day, I learned the truth: my uncle had passed away during the night the horses had visited me. The memory of the dream and the news fused instantly. From that moment, I could not separate them. It felt as though some part of me had already known—that my subconscious had received a message my waking mind was not yet ready to accept.

How could this be possible? Neuroscience would say dreams are a kind of rehearsal space, where emotions and sensory fragments are stitched together. Perhaps I had sensed something in the air—subtle cues no one spoke aloud. Or perhaps, in ways beyond explanation, the bond between us crossed into my sleep and painted itself as galloping white horses. Whatever the mechanism, it was my first encounter with the mystery of grief: how the mind knows before the body can accept.

In the daylight, nothing was processed. The loss was buried, unspoken. There were no open conversations—only silence. The grief went underground, where it remained, shaping me quietly and teaching me to hide pain rather than face it.

That silence echoed for decades. It was not only my uncle I lost that night but also a piece of my innocence. Grief had arrived, and with it, a lifelong pattern: to bury what was unbearable and to carry wounds that had no voice.

When my uncle died, I lost more than a relative. To me, he had been a kind of father figure—someone steady, someone who made me feel seen in ways others did not. His absence left an emptiness I could not name at twelve years old, and without language for grief, I buried it. Yet grief has a way of leaking out, finding cracks in the walls we try to build. For me, it leaked into relationships.

Clinging out of Fear

The attachment wound began quietly. After his death, something in me grew suspicious of closeness. If someone so central could disappear so suddenly, then everyone else was only temporarily mine. I did not think this consciously as a child, but the belief settled deep, like sediment at the bottom of a river. As I grew older, that hidden conviction shaped how I reached out to people—and how I feared losing them.

With girlfriends in my teenage years and twenties, I often clung too tightly. On the surface, I carried bravado—jokes, toughness, recklessness—but beneath it was fear: fear of abandonment, fear that the person I leaned on would vanish the way my uncle had. My need for closeness could become suffocating, and when cracks appeared in the relationship, I often spiraled. It was not only about that girlfriend or that argument—it was the echo of a twelve-year-old boy losing the figure he trusted most.

There was also a strange push-and-pull. While part of me clung desperately, another part kept its guard raised. If I trusted too much,

I might be destroyed again. So I lived with contradictions: needy but distant, longing for intimacy but armored against it. I could give passion, energy, and even loyalty. Still, beneath it all was an unease I could not explain to myself, much less to anyone else.

It was only with Riina that something shifted. She was the first relationship in which the undertones of grief began to soften into trust. With her, I could let down some of the defenses. It was not immediate—trust is not rebuilt in a day—but gradually, her presence gave me a new model for attachment. She did not disappear when I expected her to. She did not punish me for my fears.

Through her, I began to see that intimacy did not have to mean loss—that love could be steady, not fragile. Her presence did not erase the wound my uncle's death had left, but it changed the way I carried it. The grief, once buried and sharp, began to integrate, to take a different shape. It became part of my story rather than a silent force dictating my relationships from underneath.

Still, I recognize now how much damage was done before I ever reached that point. For years, grief hid beneath bravado. It surfaced in the nicknames I laughed off in courtrooms, in the reckless nights that looked like freedom but were fear in disguise. I wanted to be seen as strong, unbreakable, untouchable. But inside, I was carrying attachment wounds that made every closeness feel temporary, every love precarious.

This is what grief does when it is unprocessed. It does not stay politely in the past—it seeps into the present, into the way we love, fight, and cling. The loss of my uncle taught me the fragility of bonds long before I was ready to understand it. That lesson replayed in every romance that followed. Only with time—and with the steady presence of Riina—did I begin to rewrite the script.

The Currency of Company

I see the irony of my past. I thought bravado would protect me—that if I laughed, joked, and appeared tough, no one would see the wounds. But the bravado was only a mask, and the grief leaked through anyway. It shaped me, and it shaped the way I attached to others, until I finally learned that trust was not about denying loss, but about allowing love to coexist with it.

A recurring pattern was evident: people often gathered around me not for who I was, but for what I could give. At different times, the "currency" changed–sometimes it was access, sometimes bravado, sometimes resources–but the transaction was always the same. What looked like friendship was often only a way to be used.

In my younger years, I mistook presence for loyalty. If people were near me–laughing, sharing my chaos–I thought it meant I belonged. But in truth, many were only there for what my presence offered: the distraction, the alcohol, the thrill of living at the edges. When the noise ended, so did the company. Mornings always told the truth: empty glasses on the table, an empty room, and an echoes of conversations that had dissolved into nothing.

Later, the same emptiness appeared in other forms. In certain circles, loyalty was tied to status. As long as I carried an edge–toughness, reputation, a role in someone else's story–I was surrounded. But when the edge dulled, when I no longer offered what they wanted to borrow, the crowd thinned. Applause that had seemed loud one day grew silent the next.

In life, the pattern can repeat itself. Some values skills, drive, or problem-solving–but the moment their benefit ends, so does the relationship. The applause is not for the person; it is for what the person provides.

The emotional cost of these realizations was steep. Each instance confirmed the suspicion I had carried since childhood: that I was disposable, that my worth lasted only as long as I could deliver something. That sense of being used corroded trust. I found myself questioning every gesture of closeness: Do they want me, or what I bring?

What makes this clearer now is the contrast. Because alongside those hollow loyalties, I did encounter bonds that were not transactional. With Riina and Damien, the Rottweiler, I found anchors that did not vanish when the bottles were empty, when the applause faded, when I had nothing left to offer. These relationships stayed. They filled the room with a presence that did not evaporate in the morning.

The irony is that being "used" so often eventually sharpened my ability to recognize what was real. The emptiness of those conditional ties became the backdrop against which genuine loyalty shone all the more brightly. Still, the scars remain—echoes of empty rooms, empty glasses, empty applause.

In the end, I learned that what looks like loyalty can be nothing more than noise. True belonging is quieter, steadier, and remains when the glasses are cleared away.

Neurological Scars

Unresolved grief and repeated experiences of rejection do more than leave emotional scars—they leave neurological ones. When the brain encounters loss without repair, the amygdala, which governs fear and threat detection, becomes hyperactive. This hypervigilance is the nervous system's attempt to protect against future pain, but it comes at a cost: even neutral interactions can feel like threats, and closeness can feel unsafe.

Neuroscientists have found that social pain and physical pain share overlapping neural pathways, particularly in the anterior cingulate cortex. In other words, being excluded or abandoned activates the same brain circuits as a physical injury. This is why rejection "hurts" in a literal sense, and why attachment wounds can be so destabilizing.

When grief is buried instead of processed, the brain strengthens the circuits of mistrust and isolation. Each new disappointment reinforces the pathway: connection is dangerous, belonging is temporary, trust will be broken. Over time, this wiring becomes the default. The paradox, however, is that the brain is plastic—capable of change. With safe relationships, reflection, and repair, those same circuits can be rewired toward trust. But until then, the amygdala keeps scanning—always on alert, always braced for the next loss.

The uncle's absence, the feeling of being used by peers, and the lack of solid role models were never isolated events. At the time, I tried to compartmentalize them—a death here, a betrayal there, a silence where guidance should have been. But looking back, I can see they braided together into a single thread that wound itself through my life: distrust.

Each experience reinforced the same message. Losing my uncle taught me that people could vanish without warning. Being exploited by peers taught me that loyalty could be an illusion, that a company could evaporate the moment I had nothing left to offer. And the absence of steady role models left me without anyone to counter those lessons, no voice to tell me that trust could survive grief or that loyalty could be genuine.

What I carried forward was not only the pain of those moments, but also their echo. The echo whispered into every new relationship, every group I entered, every risk of closeness I considered. It was not the events themselves I was surviving—it was the reverberations, the aftershocks that kept replaying long after the moment had passed.

The lesson for me now is clear: trauma rarely exists in isolation. It compounds. One absence, one betrayal, or one silence is survivable. But when woven together, they become a narrative that the mind begins to accept as truth. For years, my truth was that trust was dangerous and belonging was temporary.

If I Could Speak to My Younger Self

The Dream of the White Horses Was Your First Encounter with Grief

It was not imagination; it was your mind's way of telling you that something precious was leaving. You did not have the tools to process it then, but your subconscious was already whispering what words could not.

Silence Buries Pain but Never Erases It

You pushed grief down because no one gave you language for it. But buried wounds still leak out. They shaped your fear of abandonment, your bravado, and your mistrust. I would tell you: speak it; do not hide it.

Attachment Wounds Replay Themselves

Your uncle's death was not just the loss of a loved one; it was the seed of suspicion toward closeness. Later, with girlfriends, you clung too tightly and pulled away at the same time. That contradiction was not weakness—it was grief repeating itself.

Being "Used" Is Not the Same As Being Valued

The peers who showed up for the beer, the noise, and the status—they were not loyal to you, only to what you could provide. Empty rooms and empty glasses are not measures of your worth.

Real Anchors Exist

Riina's patience, Damien's loyalty, and Pulla's presence—these were not conditional. They did not disappear when you had nothing left to give. They proved that love can be steady.

Trauma Compounds into Distrust, but It Can Be Rewired

Grief, betrayal, and the absence of role models braided together into a thread of distrust that shaped your life for years. But the brain is plastic: with trust, reflection, and repair, those circuits can change.

The Echo Is Not the Truth

You were not surviving events; you were surviving their echoes. And echoes fade. The past is not destiny.

When Thrill Became Emptiness

I woke in a round room where the walls were padded, their seams stitched with silence, and cameras watched from the upper corners like unblinking eyes. I was lying on a thin yellow mattress, its plastic cover clinging to the air with the faint, synthetic smell of cardboard and hospital disinfectant. The quiet was not peaceful but oppressive—so heavy it seemed to press against my ears until even the distant sound of doors slamming in the corridor felt like thunder. Voices came and went, muffled, detached, reminders that the world continued beyond this padded cell.

I felt strange in my own body, caught between two realities: one blurred by the psychosis, and the other dulled by medication. Only a day earlier, I had been brought here, into the surveillance room of the mental hospital, and now I floated somewhere between paranoia and emptiness.

Oddly, shame was not the strongest emotion. Instead, there was hollowness, as though my fractured mind had somehow stumbled back into itself, returning home not with relief but with exhaustion. The day before, everything had been different: paranoia burned through me, convincing me that my closest friends had conspired against me, that betrayal was everywhere. In that moment, the delusion felt absolute, as real as the mattress beneath me.

This was not my first journey into such altered states, but something in me shifted this time. For the first time, I could see, however faintly, the tricks my mind was capable of playing. I began to recognize the shape of the illusions—how they grew out of old wounds, years of stress, substances, and the restless environment I had built around myself.

Lying there on the yellow mattress, I began to understand that psychosis was not a storm that came from nowhere. It was a mirror, reflecting back the chaos I had carried for years.

Finding My Fix

When I look back, much of my life appears as a series of attempts to medicate feelings I could not face. Pride, anxiety, shame, and grief—each one demanded a fix. And I had a fix ready: beer, amphetamines, steroids, and food. They were my shortcuts to survival—my quick hits of dopamine and adrenaline. But each "solution" carried its own cost.

Beer was pride in liquid form. With a drink in my hand, I could laugh louder, speak bolder, play the role of the strong man who never bent. Alcohol dulled self-consciousness and quieted the gnawing suspicion that I was still that outsider boy who did not belong. For a few hours, I could be the version of myself I wanted others to see. But when the buzz faded, the pride collapsed, leaving a deeper shame than before.

Amphetamines and sometimes cocaine were my answer to anxiety. When restlessness and doubt tightened around me, speed gave me focus, energy, and the illusion of control. The adrenaline rush made me feel as if I could outrun anything—failure, fear, even myself. But the crash always came. What started as a shield against worry left me with even more jagged nerves, a body that could not rest, and a mind that mistrusted its own silence.

Steroids were the mask I wore over shame. They promised strength, stature, and an armor the world could see. Muscles became my argument against vulnerability—my way of proving I was untouchable. But it was a fragile armor. The stronger I looked, the weaker I felt inside.

And then there was food—my comfort against grief. When sadness pressed in, I turned to excess: pizza, chocolate, and kebab—meals not of nourishment but of numbing. The rush of calories was a brief distraction, a heaviness in the stomach that quieted the heaviness in the heart. But overeating only layered one form of pain over another, leaving me bloated, sluggish, and buried deeper in self-contempt.

What tied all these together was dopamine and adrenaline. Each fix offered a quick jolt of chemical relief. Alcohol flooded me with the social ease I longed for. Amphetamines and cocaine triggered a rush of dopamine and adrenaline that sharpened my focus and made the world seem manageable. Steroids tapped into the brain's reward pathways, linking power and validation to the mirror's reflection.

But none of it lasted. The brain adapts. Dopamine highs always demand more the next time, and adrenaline burns the system out. What began as a fix soon became a trap. Each time, the void I tried to fill grew larger, not smaller. Pride gave way to humiliation. Anxiety came back sharper. Shame grew heavier.

The difference, I now understand, is between survival fixes and lasting nourishment. Survival fixes are quick, frantic attempts to push pain aside. They work in the moment, but erode the foundation underneath. Lasting nourishment, on the other hand, takes time, patience, and honesty. It does not silence pain; it gives pain space to be faced and eventually transformed.

For years, I thought I was filling a hole inside me with these substances and habits. In truth, I was digging it deeper. Beer, pill, injection, and binge were shovels in my own hands. The more I tried to patch over the void, the wider and darker it became.

It took me a long time to see this clearly—to realize that what I thought were solutions were symptoms, proof of wounds I had never allowed to heal. Pride, anxiety, shame, and grief: they demanded more than a fix. They demanded acknowledgement, processing, and compassion. Only then could the chasing stop and real nourishment begin.

Freedom Without Anchor

At fifteen, I thought I had found liberation. Moving into my own apartment was supposed to mean freedom—a boy's dream of independence made real. No one to judge me, no one to tell me what to do. For a while, I wore that freedom like armor.

But the armor cracked quickly. Freedom without anchors is not safety; it is exposure. Alone in those rooms, silence pressed in until it became suffocating. I felt it staring through the Shell station window at night, watching fluorescent light spill over empty asphalt. I felt it in a Lidl doorway, pretending to wait for someone when in truth I was stalling, afraid of going back to the hollow apartment. Later, in the padded camera room of the psychiatric ward, silence was no longer emptiness but surveillance—a reminder of how exposed I truly was.

And then came the visions.

It was a Friday night, after a long snooze following amphetamine use, when the skeletons crawled out of my mind. I lay on the sofa and saw them move across the walls—grotesque creatures with human lower bodies and skeletal upper torsos, bone-white and jerking as though half alive, half dead. At first, I laughed. "Nice tricks, mind," I thought. But then they multiplied. Black figures, shadow-like, darted across the corners of my apartment. I got up and tried to catch them, even though some part of me knew they were not real. Adrenaline surged; my heart raced.

What struck me most was not the visions themselves but my reaction. I was not consumed by fear. Instead, I experienced a strange rush—part curiosity, part adrenaline. The body responds to psychosis much like it does to danger: the heart races, the senses sharpen, and the world tilts into hyper-awareness. Adrenaline pushes the system into overdrive. But in my case, that chemical storm collided with the awareness that these visions were illusions.

Analyzing it now, I can see the chemistry behind it. Amphetamines spike dopamine, flooding the reward pathways and overwhelming the brain's natural balance. My system was already under strain from years of stress and exhaustion. With that extra chemical push, the line between reality and illusion collapsed. The psychotic episode was not random—it was my brain firing in overdrive, with dopamine amplifying both my paranoia and my imagination.

But not all episodes were tied to substances. Once, while watching television, I saw the text on the screen duplicate itself—two lines where there should have been one. That moment did not come from drugs; it came from something deeper—the heavy load of chronic stress, the long-term toll of exhaustion, isolation, and unresolved grief. Neuroscience would say the stress had primed my amygdala into hypervigilance, while cortisol and dopamine circuits tangled until perception itself began to fracture.

So, what was the root? In one sense, chemicals—amphetamines, adrenaline, dopamine surges. In another, something far more fundamental: the collapse of a boy's freedom fantasy. I had built my independence on sand. Instead of structure, I had silence. Instead of anchors, I had hallucinations.

Here is the cruel paradox: adrenaline made those visions feel alive. The body treated them like danger—pumping blood faster, sharpening focus, urging me to act. In that storm, even illusions became companions. Chasing shadows across my living room was easier than sitting in the stillness of loneliness. Psychosis became a twisted form of company.

The lesson came later. Freedom, as I once imagined it, was a lie. True freedom does not come from isolation, from pushing the world away. Without anchors—love, trust, and belonging—solitude turns toxic. Independence without connection is not liberation but emptiness—the kind of emptiness that invites skeletons onto the walls and shadows into the corners.

What I thought was freedom at fifteen was actually the start of collapse. No amount of adrenaline, dopamine, or hallucinated company could protect me from the truth. Without anchors, freedom becomes another prison—one you build yourself.

Chronic stress leaves fingerprints on the brain. One of its most striking effects is on the hippocampus—the region responsible for memory and perspective. When cortisol levels remain elevated for too long, hippocampal volume begins to shrink. As a result, the brain loses its ability to see time in proportion. The future becomes blurred, and the present—whether pain, fear, or emptiness—feels as if it will last forever.

Dopamine tells another part of the story. Amphetamines, alcohol, and even food binges hijack the dopamine system, flooding the brain with artificial highs. At first, the surge brings euphoria and energy. But over time, the brain adapts by downregulating receptors, leaving the system depleted. What once felt electric becomes flat. The same beer, the same pill, the same binge no longer delivers, and the void grows larger.

Oxytocin, often called the "bonding hormone," plays a quiet but vital role here. Trust, mentoring relationships, or even the unconditional loyalty of an animal can release oxytocin, buffering the effects of stress. Without it, the brain defaults to survival mode—scanning for threats, mistrusting others, and bracing for abandonment. In a life without safe anchors, survival reactivity becomes the baseline, and every interaction is filtered through vigilance rather than connection.

And then there is adrenaline. Short bursts of it can sharpen focus and heighten performance—the thrill before a fight, the clarity in an emergency. But when life becomes a constant adrenaline chase, the nervous system wears thin. What once felt like energy mutates into restlessness, insomnia, and paranoia. The body becomes addicted to its own chemistry, mistaking chaos for aliveness. This explains why illusions can feel strangely compelling.

In combination, these factors create a dangerous cycle: stress shrinks perspective, dopamine depletion flattens reward, the absence of oxytocin erodes trust, and adrenaline becomes the false fuel that keeps everything moving. Together, these factors do not describe a brain in survival mode—they describe a life trapped in it.

Survival had carried me through more than I once thought possible. It took me through rock bottoms that should have broken me, through hospital stays, prison gates, and psychotic nights that blurred the line between illusion and reality. Again and again, I stumbled forward when collapse seemed inevitable. On the surface, that was resilience. But resilience can be deceptive. Surviving the events was only half the story.

Rock bottoms can break bones, but fallout breaks something less visible and more corrosive: trust in yourself. When shame burrows into the body, when mistrust becomes your default lens, when grief leaks into relationships—survival alone is not enough. You may have made it through the night, but you wake in the morning still hollowed out, convinced you are disposable and still at war with your own mind. That is where the real damage lives.

Stumbling Forward or Rebuilding?

For years, I mistook that hollowness for strength. I thought that pushing forward meant I had won, that bravado could cover the cracks. But what I learned was to wear masks—the strong man, the untouchable man, the provider of chaos and noise. The masks worked long enough to fool others—and sometimes even myself—but they could not erase the truth. The fallout followed me into every room, every relationship, and every silence I tried to escape.

I can see now that survival was not the destination; it was a holding pattern. I had survived what I had done—the choices, the reckless years, the substances—but I had not confronted what those years had done to me. That is the difference between stumbling forward and rebuilding.

To rebuild, I needed to look beyond the events themselves and into the shadow they had cast over my inner life. I needed to face the echo, the mistrust, and the way my own brain had rewired itself to expect betrayal and emptiness. Without that confrontation, survival would always collapse back into the same patterns.

And then came the day that woke me up. A day when the echo could no longer be ignored, when survival finally gave way to something else. That day marked the threshold—not the end of struggle, but the beginning of change.

That is where Chapter Six begins.

If I Could Speak to My Younger Self

Psychosis Was a Mirror, Not a Storm

The padded room, the yellow mattress, even the skeletons crawling on the wall—they were not random. They reflected the chaos you had carried for years: stress, substances, and isolation. Your brain was not betraying you; it was showing you the cost of how you lived.

Fixes Are Not Nourishment

Beer to cover pride, amphetamines to outrun anxiety, steroids to mask shame, and food to numb grief—each of them felt like relief, but none of them healed. They were survival shortcuts. Every fix deepened the hole instead of filling it.

Dopamine and Adrenaline Lie

The rush of alcohol, the jolt of amphetamines, and even the thrill of chasing hallucinations—they convinced you that life was manageable, maybe even exciting. But the brain adapts. Highs flatten, adrenaline exhausts, and soon you are left emptier than before. The chemistry was never on your side.

Freedom Without Anchors Is Exposure

At fifteen, you thought independence was liberation. But solitude turned toxic. Shell station windows, Lidl doorways, psychiatric wards–the silence in all of them proved that freedom without love, trust, or belonging is just another prison.

Stress Rewires the Brain

Chronic cortisol shrinks perspective, making "now" feel endless. Without oxytocin–trust, mentors, and safe bonds–the brain defaults to hypervigilance, bracing for betrayal. That is why connection felt unsafe, even when you longed for it.

Survival Is Not the Same as Rebuilding

You stumbled forward through rock bottoms, convinced that not collapsing was enough. But survival was only a holding pattern. The real damage was emotional fallout: mistrust, shame, and hollowed-out mornings. To heal, you needed to confront not what you had done but what it had done to you.

Change Begins When Survival Is No Longer Enough

Masks and bravado could hide the cracks for a while–but not forever. Eventually, survival had to give way to something else: the choice to rebuild, to find anchors, and to trust again.

PART TWO

THE AWAKENING

CHAPTER 6

The Day That Woke Me Up

A Chance Encounter That Changed Everything

Looking back, I see a clear difference between these encounters and the ones I ignored before. The math teacher who came to the prison, the sergeant who saw my restlessness, and the nurse who asked about my sleep–they had all offered me guidance. But at the time, I was deaf to it. Survival mode does not allow for nuance; it only scans for threats or rewards. Anything in between was filtered out as irrelevant noise.

By 2013 and 2014, I was frayed. The chaos, the psychosis, and the endless loop of substances had stripped me down. I was not ready in the sense of seeking change, but I was porous in a way I had not been before. Riina's steady gaze landed differently because my defenses were thinner. My friend's blunt words stung because my ego had fewer shields left to protect it.

I think the moment in my home with the skeletons–especially when I realized I was in psychosis and could name it–had something to do with this new openness. That shock of clarity, of seeing myself from the outside, tore a hole in the old script. From then on, some part of me knew I could not keep everything shut out.

These fragments mattered because they arrived in a season when I could no longer pretend that survival was working. My old strategies–denial, bravado, and numbing–had failed often enough to create cracks. And cracks, painful as they are, let light in.

The encounters themselves were not dramatic. They were casual, quiet, and almost forgettable. But precisely because of that, they were believable. They did not demand that I reinvent myself on the spot; they showed me another possibility. These were the beginnings of pivots–not because the world around me changed, but because, for the first time, I started to let something in.

When Riina looked me in the eyes in December 2013, it was not the gaze of someone judging me or dismissing me. It was steady, patient, and curious–a kind of attention I had not felt since my uncle took me fishing as a child. The timing was everything. Earlier in my life, I would have brushed her off or drowned the feeling in noise. But now, depleted and raw, that simple presence hit differently.

The same goes for my friend's blunt words: "Your psyche can't handle substances anymore." We were not in a living room or a bar. We were standing in a narrow aisle leading to the gym, our voices echoing off concrete walls. The only background sound was water moving through the pipes above us–a hollow, steady trickle that seemed to underline his words. Ten years earlier, I would have laughed it off, turned it into a joke, or found a way to prove him wrong by doubling down. But in that corridor, his words landed differently. My chest tightened, and though I smirked on the outside, inside, I felt something breaking open. The armor that had once shielded me from all criticism was already thin from psychosis, hospital stays, and endless chaos. That simple line became the seed of long-term sobriety, even if it took years to sprout. For the first time, someone had named aloud what my body already knew.

Even in prison, when a teacher laid down a math problem and waited silently, it felt different from all the classrooms before. I was not the loud, disruptive boy trying to score dopamine hits by making the class laugh. I was not the dropout sneaking out of school for cigarettes. I was a man in a cell, with a sheet of paper, being asked to try. His silence was not condemnation, not shame, but invitation. Earlier in life, I had ignored mentors: the sergeant who told me I was always looking sideways, the nurse who asked if I was sleeping, and the teachers who tried to give me tools. Survival mode had filtered them out as irrelevant because I did not yet feel the need to hear them.

The difference was not that these people were more brilliant or more caring than those who came before. The difference was me. I had reached a state where my walls had cracks and where survival mode had run its course. When survival stops delivering, the mind finally begins to search for something else. That "something else" arrived in these fragments of presence, honesty, and patience.

That is why these encounters mattered. They did not rescue or fix me. They landed—and stayed—where earlier lessons had bounced off.

Arriving Like Ripples

The changes did not arrive like fireworks; they arrived like ripples on water. Each encounter left a small mark, and only later did I realize that they were part of a wider pattern.

One of the earliest ripples came inside prison walls. Exercise had always been a way to feed my pride—to bulk up with steroids and display muscles as armor. But behind bars, where substances were stripped away and choices were limited, exercise became something different. It was no longer about intimidation; it was about rhythm, discipline, and feeling alive in a body that had nearly killed itself. I began to notice the difference between chasing size and chasing strength, between looking powerful and becoming resilient.

Meeting Riina brought another ripple. At first, I did not know what to make of her calm steadiness. I was used to chaos: friends who disappeared when the party was over, lovers who collided with my fears of abandonment, and circles where loyalty lasted only as long as the bottle did. But Riina was not swayed by those games. She did not need me to be the strongest, the funniest, or the wildest. What she reflected to me was something I had not known before: stability. Through her, I began to see that a relationship could be more than adrenaline or escape. It could be a mirror that showed me who I was—and who I could become if I stopped running. Even her dog, Mr. Damien, leaning his weight against me with quiet trust, felt like a test I wanted to pass.

Studying in prison added another ripple. When that teacher handed me math problems, I felt something unfamiliar: patience. For once, I was not trying to escape the room, outwit the system, or grab quick rewards. I was simply solving, step by step. That rhythm of numbers steadied me. Psychology textbooks then opened another window: I began to recognize my own patterns on the page. Words like "shame," "addiction," and "trauma" no longer felt abstract; they described the currents that had pulled me under. With each chapter, I began to ask new questions.

There was also a subtler shift happening inside me: I began to revisit the events of my former life through a different lens. Moments that had once seemed like random disasters began to look like warnings. The psychosis in 2014 was no longer an embarrassing breakdown—it was proof that my brain had limits I could not keep pushing. The ICU episode after my surgery was not a medical accident—it was a reminder of how fragile life is. Even the humiliating nickname "Balloon," given when I weighed 147 kilos, now sounded less like an insult and more like a signal that my body was buckling under pressure. These memories began to change shape in my mind.

None of these changes was dramatic at first. But together, they began to shift the current. What once felt like an endless cycle of survival started, slowly, to look like the beginning of a new direction.

Chance encounters strike deeper when the ground beneath you is already shaking. A healthy, stable person might hear a blunt comment or meet someone new and walk away unchanged. But when you are stripped raw—exhausted, paranoid, and fractured by years of chaos—your brain is strangely receptive. The walls that once filtered out every piece of advice are thinner. That is why Riina's gaze, my friend's blunt line in the gym corridor, and even the quiet patience of a prison teacher landed where earlier voices had bounced off.

The science backs this up. During times of crisis, neuroplasticity–the brain's ability to rewire and form new pathways–is heightened. Stress hormones flood the system, but if a person encounters safety, honesty, or connection in that fragile window, the nervous system can latch onto it. Honest words act like a reset signal; safe relationships release oxytocin, calming the hyperactive fear circuits; and small achievements, like solving a math problem, spark dopamine in a healthier and steadier way than drugs ever did. These encounters are not magic. They are catalysts–openings where the brain, desperate for stability, accepts a new script.

For me, one of the strongest catalysts was not a conversation but a realization. In the middle of a psychotic episode in 2014, I suddenly understood that I was in psychosis. It was as if I stepped outside myself for a moment and saw the state I was in. That clarity did not end the episode, but it changed my relationship to it. It was no longer chaos; it was a condition, something with a name. That naming gave me a sliver of control. Psychosis usually drowns a person in confusion, but recognizing it gave me a thin thread to hold on to.

I believe that moment cracked something open in me. It was the first time I saw my mind as separate from the storm it was generating. That gap–between "me" and the psychosis–was painful, but it was also powerful. It meant I could observe, not be swept away. Later, when my friend told me my psyche could not handle substances anymore, those words landed on soil that had already been broken open by the realization in the psych ward.

Reflection makes the point clearer: encounters do not transform us on their own. They present us with possibilities. It is up to us to decide what to do with them. When Riina entered my life, I could have dismissed her stability as boring. When my friend spoke in the gym corridor, I could have laughed and carried on. When the teacher handed me math problems, I could have walked away.

The lesson is simple but not easy: small cracks let light in. It was not the grand gestures or the dramatic rescues that changed my trajectory. It was the quiet, almost forgettable moments. That choice—fragile and inconsistent as it was—became the hinge that allowed survival to turn into the first glimpses of living.

These encounters did not save me outright. They did not erase the years of chaos, the scars of psychosis, or the weight of shame. What they did was shift my angle of vision—sometimes only by a fraction. But even a fraction is enough to change the path of a life over time.

The truth is that transformation rarely starts with revolutions. It begins with ripples, with fragments, and with the courage to let something—or someone—in. And once those cracks appeared, I could no longer unsee the possibility of change.

The real change began when I looked at the same life through a different lens. They were not just scars to be hidden—they were messages waiting to be heard. I began asking the right questions: What if my life did not have to be defined by survival? What if I could actually choose a strategy, not just stumble forward?

Survival is not the end—it is the opening.

If I Could Talk to My Younger Self

Survival Mode Deafens You

If I could talk to my younger self, I would remind him of something he could not see back then: survival mode deafens you. When you are scanning only for threats or rewards, everything in between—the teacher's patience, the sergeant's warning, and the nurse's concern—registers as noise. You miss guidance not because it is not there, but because your brain has no room for nuance.

When the Armor Cracks

By 2013 and 2014, though, the armor was cracking. Chaos, psychosis, and endless substances had stripped me down to raw nerve. I was not "ready for change" in the heroic sense—but I was porous. Words and looks that once bounced off now found a way in. A friend's blunt honesty in a gym corridor, Riina's steady gaze across a December night, and even a math problem on a sheet of prison paper—they all landed because my defenses were thinner.

Cracks Are Invitations

I would tell my younger self that the cracks were not weakness—they were invitations. The shock of recognizing I was in psychosis, of naming it while still inside it, was proof that awareness could grow even in the darkest state. Those fragments did not save me outright, but they shifted my angle just enough to show another way.

Seeing My Life Through a Different Lens

The cell was quiet except for the faint metallic echo of keys somewhere down the corridor. I sat at the narrow desk—the kind of furniture meant more for storage than study—with a paperback psychology book opens in front of me. The bars on the window cast striped shadows across the page, and for once, they did not feel like barriers. They felt like markers, as if the light itself was dividing the past from what might still be ahead.

I traced a sentence with my finger, reading it over and over: self-esteem develops through consistent feedback and a secure environment. The words stung—they described exactly what I had lacked, but they also gave me language for it. For the first time, my chaos was not just chaos—it was something I could study, name, and maybe even change.

The routines of prison were still there: the clang of gates, the same faces at exercise, and the slow march of days. But something in me shifted. When I solved a math problem later that week, it was not just numbers on a page; it was proof that I could still learn and still build something brick by brick, even inside concrete walls.

It was not freedom in the usual sense, but it was a different kind of freedom—a freedom of perspective.

For the first time, I began to see that the same life—viewed through a different lens—could tell an entirely new story.

Until prison, my life had been a chain of reactions: someone laughed, and I acted out; someone offered drugs, and I said yes; survival required an immediate fix, and I delivered. I never had the space or tools to pause, reflect, or name what was actually happening inside me. That changed the day I picked up a high school psychology book in my cell.

Math and Psychology as New Paths

At first, I read it like any other book, my eyes moving over the text without much expectation. But soon, the words started to hit differently. Shame. Anxiety. Grief. These were not abstract academic terms—they were fingerprints on my own life. For years, I had thought of my shame as weakness, something to be hidden. In psychology, I learned it was a universal response, wired into us to protect our social bonds. My constant anxiety, which had driven me to scan every room for threats, was no longer a mysterious curse. It was hypervigilance, a nervous system stuck in survival mode. And grief—the heaviness I never allowed myself to feel when my uncle died—suddenly had a name, a shape, and a legitimacy.

Naming emotions gave me distance from them. Instead of being swallowed whole by shame or anxiety, I could say, this is shame; this is what my body does when I feel it. That simple reframing changed everything. Once I could recognized the pattern, I could start working with it rather than against it. My inner world shifted from chaos to something I could map. For the first time, I felt like I was getting to know myself in a way that might lead somewhere.

Math, oddly enough, did the same kind of work on a different level. When a teacher came into the prison once a week and handed us problem sets, I expected boredom. Instead, I found something steadying. Each equation was a puzzle that did not care about my past, my crimes, or my shame. The answer was either correct or incorrect, and progress came one step at a time. There were no shortcuts, no way to fake it with bravado or charm. To solve a problem, I had to sit still, concentrate, and trust the process.

That discipline seeped into me slowly. Where my old life was about instant gratification—beer for courage, amphetamines for focus, and steroids for confidence—math demanded patience. The joy came not from the immediate hit, but from the slow build: a concept understood, a formula applied, a result checked and confirmed. Each small success reminded me that progress was possible, but only if I stayed with the work.

Together, psychology and math offered me two lenses. Psychology gave me the language for my emotions—tools to decode shame, anxiety, and grief, and a clear frame to understand my mind. Math gave me the structure—a way to practice patience, to see that long-term effort could actually lead to long-term results. Between the two, survival started to look less like a constant scramble and more like something that could be shaped into a strategy.

It was a revelation: maybe life did not have to be an endless chain of reactions. Maybe I could plan, prepare, and act with intention. The idea of "strategy" had always felt out of reach—like something for people with normal childhoods, safe homes, or higher education. But here I was in a prison cell, learning that strategy could start with something as small as naming an emotion or solving for x.

The more I studied, the more I recognized patterns from my past. I saw how shame had driven me into hiding, how anxiety had sharpened me into paranoia, and how grief had left me numb. But instead of letting those forces define me, I began to see them as signals. If shame made me want to withdraw, maybe I could choose a different response. If anxiety made me scan for danger, maybe I could ground myself in the present. If grief made me numb, maybe I could acknowledge it instead of burying it under substances. One major breakthrough was realizing that my own mind can be my best ally or my worst enemy.

This was not a clean or immediate transformation. Some days, the old habits roared back louder than ever. But the difference was that I now had a map. For the first time, I could see where I was— even if I was not yet where I wanted to be.

That is why I say prison was where survival first began to turn into strategy. Not because the system offered me perfect rehabilitation— it didn't. Not because I suddenly became disciplined and sober—I hadn't. But because, for the first time, I realized there was another way to live, and I had the tools to start experimenting with it.

Those hours with psychology textbooks and math problems were more than study sessions. They were rehearsals for a different kind of life—one where I was not just reacting but actually choosing. They taught me that even in the narrowest of places, the mind can expand. And once the mind expands, it is hard to shrink it back to the old dimensions.

The ripple effect of those lessons carried far beyond the prison gates. They did not erase the past or guarantee the future, but they marked the beginning of something crucial: the shift from being a survivor of circumstances to becoming a strategist of my own life.

The Tide Has Turned

The biggest shift that came with reframing was how I saw myself. For years, my identity was built on being the outsider. I was the boy without a father, the teenager with no boundaries, and the young man who never quite belonged. That label followed me everywhere. It colored how I read other people's reactions, how I walked into rooms, and even how I sabotaged opportunities.

Being the outsider became both shield and excuse: if I did not belong, then nothing was really expected of me.

That old story started to lose its hold. I could see that my struggles were not just proof of exclusion—they were evidence of survival. I had carried shame, anxiety, and grief without the tools to process them. I had endured toxic environments and dangerous circles. I had lived through psychosis, overdoses, broken relationships, and still I was here, sitting at a desk, turning pages, solving problems. Outsider was no longer the right word. Survivor was.

That small but powerful reframe lifted my self-esteem in a way steroids or bravado never could. Steroids had built temporary confidence; drugs had created a false illusion of being in control of my own life; and alcohol had given me an escape from this dimension for a few hours. But they all collapsed the moment reality returned. Survivor, on the other hand, was a lasting identity. It was rooted not in illusion but in fact: I had endured. And if I could survive, maybe I could also grow.

Another payoff came in how I processed emotions. In the past, my default was to numb—to drink when shame hit, to snort when anxiety surged, and to binge on food when grief crept in. Each of those choices pushed the feelings out of sight, but they never disappeared. They only built pressure, waiting for the next eruption.

Through study and reflection, I began to experiment with something new: letting emotions pass through me. Instead of clinging to them or pushing them away, I learned to notice them. Sadness could be acknowledged without drowning in it. Shame could be recognized without letting it drive me into hiding. Anxiety could be felt in the body—the tight jaw, the racing heart—and then released with breath and movement.

I developed what I think of as a "positive mind" approach. It was not about pretending everything was fine or forcing fake optimism. It was about trusting that feelings were temporary, that they did not define me unless I let them. By allowing them to flow through, rather than sticking or festering, I created space inside myself. I stopped fearing my own emotions.

Even prison itself changed meaning once I looked through this new lens. Before, I had only seen it as punishment and wasted years—and in many ways, it was punishment. But it was also an opportunity. With fewer distractions and with the chaos of my old life stripped away, I had the time and silence to study, to exercise, and to reflect. Prison became a laboratory of sorts—not one I would wish for, but one that gave me room to test new ways of thinking and feeling.

The emotional payoff was freedom of a different kind—not the freedom of open doors or unlocked gates, but the freedom of no longer being enslaved to my old patterns. I no longer had to run from shame, numb grief, or hide from anxiety. I could let them arrive, pass through me, and leave without destroying me. That gave me resilience.

In the end, the shift was not about erasing pain but about transforming its role. Pain was no longer just an enemy; it became information. My outsider story had locked me into cycles of self-doubt and self-destruction, but my survivor story gave me permission to see pain as part of growth. And that perspective, more than any sentence or system, marked the beginning of real change.

Reframing Your Story

Reframing your story is not just a mental trick—it physically reshapes the brain. When you live in survival mode, the limbic system (the emotional brain) runs the show. Stress hormones like cortisol keep the body on alert, while the prefrontal cortex—the part of the brain responsible for planning, long-term thinking, and self-control—goes partly offline. That is why so many of my past choices felt impulsive: I was not thinking about tomorrow; I was only thinking about the next ten minutes.

When I began to reframe myself from "outsider" to "survivor," something shifted in those circuits. Naming shame, anxiety, and grief engaged the prefrontal cortex again. Each time I said, this is shame, not me, I was pulling decision-making power back from the emotional brain and giving it to the part of me that could strategize.

The dopamine system also began to change. Before, I chased quick chemical highs—beer, amphetamines, steroids, and sugar. They spiked dopamine like fireworks: sudden, dazzling, but gone in seconds, leaving only darkness. With reframing, the same dopamine reward system started to respond to different cues: finishing a math problem, reading a psychology chapter, or exercising without steroids. These rewards were more like a campfire—smaller, steadier, and capable of keeping me warm for the long night ahead.

That is the science of reframing: it does not erase old circuits, but it lays down new ones strong enough to carry a different life forward.

Changing my lens did not erase the past. The blackouts, the psychosis, the broken relationships, and the endless drift—none of that disappeared when I picked up a psychology book or solved a math problem. What changed was the meaning I gave those scars. Instead of proof that I was worthless, they became evidence that I had survived. Instead of endless reasons to hide, they became blueprints for how I could build differently.

Reframing was not about denying the pain; it was about placing it in context. Shame showed me how deeply I had craved connection. Anxiety revealed how hard my mind worked to protect me. Even grief, numbed for years, reminded me of the capacity I had to love in the first place. Each emotion, once an enemy, became a kind of raw material—jagged, yes, but useful if I learned how to shape it.

That shift was only a beginning. Survival had become a strategy, but a strategy was not yet a full life. The next step was to stop running from myself and to start listening inward, no matter what I found there.

With a new lens, even survival scars became blueprints. The next question was how to build something lasting from them.

Me and Mr Damien.

If I Could Talk to My Younger Self

Survival Mode Is Not Living

If I could talk to my younger self, I would tell him that survival mode is not living—it is reacting. Back then, every choice was a chain reaction: someone laughed and you acted out; someone offered drugs and you said yes; someone challenged you and you fought. It felt like freedom, but it was only a reflex. Survival mode scans for threats and quick rewards—everything else, including the teacher's patience, the sergeant's warning, and the nurse's question, was filtered out as irrelevant noise.

Cracks Are Invitations

I would tell him that the cracks—the moments when you felt exhausted, ashamed, or lost—were not weaknesses; they were invitations. When Riina looked at you in 2013, when a friend's blunt words echoed in a gym corridor, or when a prison teacher slid a math problem across the desk, those were not ordinary moments. They landed differently because your defenses were thin. For the first time, you let something in.

Emotions Are Signals, Not Curses

I would tell him that shame, anxiety, and grief were not curses; they were signals. With language from psychology, you could name them. With patience in math, you could endure them. With reframing, you could turn them from enemies into teachers.

Scars Are Evidence of Survival

And finally, I would tell him this: your scars are not proof that you are broken; they are evidence that you have survived. Once you see yourself as a survivor, strategy becomes possible. Even prison bars can become blueprints if you choose the right lens.

CHAPTER 7

Choosing to Look Inward

The Beginning of Self-Examination

The first steps into self-examination were awkward, hesitant, and clumsy—but they were steps all the same. For most of my life, reflection had been a foreign concept. My default had been action: drink, fight, escape, and repeat. If anything resembling self-awareness appeared, I drowned it with substances before it could grow teeth. But prison stripped away the quick fixes, leaving me face to face with myself in ways I could no longer avoid.

It began with a book. I read it the way you flip through a manual for a machine you do not expect to repair. But then certain words began to stick: shame, anxiety, and grief. They were not just academic concepts; they were fingerprints all over my own life. For years, I had treated shame as proof of weakness, anxiety as a private curse, and grief as something to bury so deep that no one could find it. Reading those terms in black and white gave them shape, legitimacy, and even a kind of neutrality. They were not punishments; they were human responses.

The act of naming them changed how I felt about them. I could now say: This is shame; this is anxiety; this is grief. Instead of drowning inside them, I could step back far enough to see their outlines. Naming became a form of power. It did not erase the emotions, but it gave me distance from them—enough space to begin making choices rather than acting on reflexes.

Journaling came next. At first, my scribbles were barely coherent: fragments of thought, angry sentences, unfinished questions. But over time, those scribbles became something more. On paper, I found a mirror. The journal was not a teacher or a critic; it simply reflected back what I poured into it. Some entries were furious, some mournful, and some confused. But when I returned to them later, I could see patterns. I began to notice how the same triggers produced the same reactions. I saw cycles of anger, shame, and avoidance repeating in loops. That recognition was a small victory. Awareness did not break the cycle instantly, but it exposed the gears turning inside it.

Exercise, too, shifted meaning during this period. For years, the gym had been a place to inflate myself—more muscle, more size, more armor against the world. Steroids and bravado had made the barbell a stage. In prison, stripped of those enhancements, every rep took on a different quality. Each set became less about intimidation and more about testing my will. Could I show up consistently? Could I push through when no one was watching? The weights measured not just strength but honesty. They revealed when I was present and when I was distracted, when I was working with intention, and when I was running on autopilot. Physical training turned into a form of introspection—a way to observe myself in real time.

Looking back, I see how all three practices—reading, writing, and moving—worked together. Psychology gave me the language, journaling gave me the mirror, and exercise gave me the test. Together, they created the beginnings of a method for self-examination.

What made this possible, though, was a skill I had first discovered in a very different context: psychosis. In 2014, when I realized mid-episode that I was in psychosis, I experienced something rare—a flash of self-observation under extreme mental distortion. For a brief moment, I could see myself from outside the storm, recognizing what was happening without being completely consumed by it. At the time, it was both amazing and strange. But later, when I studied psychology, I realized that the same ability could be cultivated in different ways. I could learn to observe my own mind not only in crisis but also in daily life. I could mirror my past and present to create impact for the future.

That skill—self-observation—became the hinge of my process. It turned the abstract into the concrete. When shame rose in my chest, I could pause and say: this is the same shame I felt in front of the class years ago. When anxiety clenched my jaw, I could recognize the same hypervigilance that kept me scanning exits in every bar. When grief numbed me, I could see that this was the same silence that swallowed me when my uncle died. By linking present feelings to past patterns, I began to map myself.

The process was not glamorous. Most nights, it was me alone at a desk under harsh fluorescent light, scribbling half-thoughts and circling words. Most days, it was me under a barbell, counting reps in my head while sweat ran into my eyes. But gradually, those small practices carved a different track in my brain. They gave me something I had never had before: the sense that I could participate in my own life instead of being dragged along by it.

Self-examination did not provide instant answers, but it did something more valuable: it introduced the possibility of choice. For a man who had lived most of his life in reflex and reaction, that possibility was revolutionary. The cell was still locked, the gates still clanged, but for the first time, I knew the real work was happening inside—not in escaping, but in observing.

Before prison, my coping mechanisms were loud, chaotic, and destructive. If shame rose in me, I reached for a bottle—drink enough, and the sting blurred into oblivion. If anxiety clenched my chest, I turned to drugs: amphetamines for focus, cannabis for laughter, and pills for sleep. If restlessness built pressure in my body, I smothered it with constant motion—driving too fast to feel the engine roar, blasting music until my ears rang, and keeping the television on through the night so silence never had a chance to settle in. Stillness felt like suffocation.

Each of these choices promised relief, and for a short while, they delivered. Alcohol numbed the ache and provided escape, drugs offered control, and motion distracted me from myself. But the crashes always came harder, leaving me emptier, more exhausted, and more alienated than before. My survival was a loop–stimulus, reaction, collapse–repeated until it almost broke me.

Inside the cell, with substances stripped away and distractions gone, I was forced into new territory. Now, the tools looked nothing like the old ones. Instead of bottles, there were books. Instead of lines on a CD case, there were lines in a notebook where I scribbled half-thoughts. Instead of noise and motion, there was silence so heavy it felt like another form of combat.

Fading the Patterns

Writing became a way to put distance between myself and my emotions. What I once drowned in beer, I now poured onto paper. Studying psychology gave me words where before there had only been static. Silence, once unbearable, became something I experimented with–though it often felt like being trapped in a room with a stranger I did not yet trust.

But the old patterns did not disappear quietly. They screamed louder than the new tools, especially in the early stages. Some nights, I could almost taste the bitterness of beer in my mouth, even though I had not touched alcohol in months. My muscles twitched with the urge to move, to drive, or to turn on a television that was not there. Sitting at a desk with a book felt pointless compared to the quick rush of substances or the false comfort of noise. The new tools seemed fragile; the old ones, solid and familiar.

The hardest part was sitting still with myself. I had to feel things raw. Shame arrived like a punch to the gut. Anxiety rattled in my bones, unchecked by chemicals. Grief, long buried, surfaced in flashes that made my throat tighten. There was no buffer, no armor, and no escape hatch–just me, a notebook, and the silence.

In those moments, the temptation to return to old coping mechanisim was fierce. But I also knew that survival mode—drink, drugs, speed, and distraction—had already failed me. It had left me in psychosis, in debt, and in prison cells. The new tools were uncomfortable, yes, but they carried a different promise: not quick relief, but the chance of a future. I was training parts of my brain that had been dormant for years. Introspection—the act of turning attention inward—is not only a psychological skill; it is a neurological exercise that reshapes the circuits we rely on to navigate life.

At the center of this shift is the prefrontal cortex, the brain's planning and decision-making hub. When life is lived in survival mode, this region is often overridden by the amygdala and other limbic structures—the emotional "survival brain." In that state, everything is reactive: fight, flight, or numb. But when I paused to name an emotion—shame, anxiety, or grief—I was re-engaging the prefrontal cortex. By labeling feelings, I gave them structure. Neuroscientists call this "affect labeling," and studies show it lowers amygdala activation. In other words, naming an emotion reduces its raw grip on the nervous system.

Another network that switched on during these moments of reflection was the default mode network (DMN)—the system active when the mind wanders, daydreams, or revisits the past. In survival mode, the DMN often loops on fear and self-criticism. But when guided through structured reflection—journaling, studying, or even reviewing my past with curiosity—the DMN becomes integrative. It weaves together memory and emotion, creating a coherent narrative instead of fragmented chaos.

This is why reflection felt so different from distraction. Driving too fast or drinking myself numb only muted symptoms for a while, but my brain stayed stuck in reactivity. Reflection, however, allowed integration. Each time I named a feeling or mapped an old behavior to a pattern, my brain was literally rewiring—strengthening connections between emotional centers and higher-order reasoning.

The shift was simple but profound: the survival brain reacts, while the self-examining brain integrates. In prison, I finally experienced the difference. For the first time, my brain was not just bracing for the next ten minutes—it was beginning to imagine the next chapter.

First Breakthrough

The first breakthrough came not from a book or a mentor, but from inside the storm itself. Recognizing what was happening while in a psychotic episode may sound small, but inside that chaos, it was like grabbing onto a rope in a flood. Naming the state did not stop it, but it gave me a thread of distance—a sliver of choice. Instead of drowning completely, I could observe myself from the outside. I realized later how rare and powerful that moment had been: the ability to self-observe, even inside madness, became a tool I could use to understand my past and navigate my future.

Another insight came to me as I looked back on my childhood. I had always felt like an outsider—the boy without a father, the kid caught in unstable homes, and the teenager who never quite fit in. For years, I thought thrill-seeking was just rebellion or fun, but in prison, I began to connect the dots. Every wild stunt, every blackout, and every risk I took was my way of compensating for that deep loneliness. Adrenaline had been a substitute for belonging. When peers cheered me on, the applause filled the same space where safety and connection should have been. Thrill-seeking was not random; it was an echo of childhood wounds I had never named.

The pattern became clearer as I examined the substances I had used. Steroids, food, alcohol—on the surface, they looked like very different choices. But when I stripped away the details, I saw they were all masks for the same wound. Steroids promised me strength when I felt weak. Food dulled the ache of grief when I could not express it. Alcohol blurred shame when it threatened to expose me. Each one was a strategy my survival brain had chosen to patch holes it did not know how to heal. They were not solutions—just costumes for pain.

These insights did not arrive like lightning bolts; they were more like puzzle pieces clicking into place. Each one gave me language and perspective I had lacked before. Realizing psychosis was a signal taught me that even in breakdown, there could be awareness. Linking outsider feelings to thrill-seeking showed me that my reckless choices were not proof of evil or stupidity—they were misguided survival tactics. All my vices were masks that revealed the common wound underneath: a craving for safety, self-worth, and connection.

Why did alcohol turn me into the opposite of who I was when sober? For a long time, I wondered why alcohol changed me so completely. Sober, I was controlled, analytical, cautious, and often withdrawn. But when I drank, I became reckless, loud, and impulsive—almost the opposite of myself. It took years of studying psychology, understanding trauma, and reflecting on my own patterns to finally understand what was happening beneath the surface.

The truth is simple: alcohol did not create a new version of me—it exposed an unregulated one.

Growing up in instability shaped my nervous system long before I took my first drink. Violence, emotional unpredictability, the absence of a stable father figure, and the feeling of being an outsider forced me to develop a survival strategy early in life. I learned to stay alert, to scan for signs of danger, to control my reactions, and to keep my emotions behind a locked door. This wasn't personality—it was protection.

Sober, that control held everything together. But alcohol disables the very part of the brain that regulates behavior: the prefrontal cortex. It shuts down the brakes.

And when those brakes disappear, what's underneath comes out.

In my case, what lay beneath was decades of suppressed emotion—anxiety, shame, anger, grief—all of it compressed into a tight core that I never learned to process. When alcohol lowered inhibition, that emotional pressure burst outward. The recklessness wasn't confidence; it was a lifetime of unprocessed feelings erupting without guidance.

And because my sober mind worked so hard to stay in control, the swing to the opposite extreme was even stronger. What I had held down so tightly came up with force.

Understanding this gave me two insights:

First, my behavior when drunk didn't mean I was a bad person. It meant I was carrying pain I never learned to handle.

Second, the key to change wasn't fighting alcohol—it was learning emotional regulation. Once I understood my own wiring, once I could sit with anxiety, shame, and grief without running, the urge to escape lost its power.

Recklessness was never the real me. It was an overflow from a nervous system trying to survive without tools. Sobriety gave me clarity, but self-examination gave me freedom.

For years, I had believed my life was just chaos—a chain of bad decisions and worse consequences. But through these small insights, I began to see a pattern. The chaos was not random—it was a survival script. And once you can name a script, you can also begin to rewrite it.

The beginning of self-examination was far from exciting. There were no grand revelations or triumphant victories. It was mostly quiet, lonely, and awkward—me sitting on a narrow prison bunk with a psychology book, scribbling half-thoughts in a notebook, or forcing myself to stay present through the burn of a workout. Often, it felt more like stumbling than progressing. The old habits screamed louder than the new ones, and the discomfort of simply sitting with myself—sober, unmasked, and without distraction— could feel unbearable.

And yet, those raw moments carried weight. For the first time, I was not only reacting—I was observing. I was learning to name them, to watch them pass through, and to see the patterns that had shaped me. Observation was not easy—rarely is—but it planted the first seed of agency.

That shift, small as it seemed, marked the real beginning of change. Self-examination did not fix everything overnight, but it gave me the first tool I truly owned: the ability to look at my life from the inside out rather than being swept away by it.

Me and Riina at the Eiffel Tower, Paris.

If I Could Talk to My Younger Self

The Awkward First Steps

If I could sit across from my younger self, I would tell him this: the first steps into self-examination will feel awkward, hesitant, and even clumsy—but they are steps all the same. For most of your life, reflection will feel foreign. Your default will be action: drink, distract, escape, and repeat. Anytime self-awareness creeps in, you will drown it with noise or substances before it grows teeth. But one day, when all the quick fixes are stripped away, you will be forced to face yourself—and that will be the beginning.

The Power of Naming

It will start with a book. Words like shame, anxiety, and grief will not just be abstract ideas—they will describe your own fingerprints. Naming them will give you power. Journaling will follow: angry fragments at first, then patterns you will begin to notice. The barbell, once armor, will become a test of honesty instead of ego.

Why Alcohol Turned Me Into the Opposite of Who I Was When Sober

Alcohol didn't turn you into someone else—it revealed the parts you had spent your whole life suppressing. Sober, you were controlled and analytical because you had to be; growing up in instability trained you to scan for danger, hold your emotions behind locked doors, and survive by staying in control. That wasn't personality; it was armor. And when alcohol shuts down your brain's brakes, the prefrontal cortex, everything you never learned to process—anxiety, shame, anger, and grief—rushed out at once. The reckless version of you wasn't a monster; he was a man carrying decades of unspoken pain with no tools to hold it.

I would tell you this, too: your behavior when drunk wasn't proof you were broken. It was proof you were overwhelmed. The real turning point came not from avoiding alcohol, but from learning emotional regulation—sitting with discomfort, naming shame, and letting grief move through you instead of drowning it. Once you stopped running from yourself, the urge to escape lost its power. Recklessness was never who you were; it was the overflow of a nervous system built for survival, not for peace. And once you learned to face what was inside you, sobriety didn't just give you clarity—it gave you freedom.

Lessons Hidden in Psychosis

Even the psychosis you fear now will later reveal itself as training: the skill of stepping outside yourself to observe. What feels like madness will plant the seed of awareness—a skill you will one day use to map the past, to steady the present, and to shape the future.

From Reactor to Observer

It will not be exciting. It will be lonely, messy, and uncomfortable. But it will also give you something you have never had before: the ability to stop reacting blindly and to start observing with intention. That shift, from reactor to observer, will change everything.

What Happens When You Stop Running

The cell door had slammed shut hours earlier, but the echo still lingered in my ears. I sat on the edge of the narrow bed, on a mattress that seemed designed more for restraint than for rest. The air was stale, tinged with disinfectant, and the only sound was the faint hum of the fluorescent light above me. No voices, no movement—just silence, heavy and unbroken.

Inside that silence, my chest tightened. Anxiety swelled first, then grief, then the old familiar sting of shame. Normally, I would have drowned them: a drink, a pill, or a workout until exhaustion—anything to chase the thoughts away. But here, in the closed prison, there was nothing to reach for. No substances, no shortcuts. Just me, locked in with emotions I had spent years outrunning.

My heart thudded so loudly I thought the guards outside might hear it. Memories pressed against me—faces I had lost, failures I could not undo, and the chaos I had created. I wanted to escape, to smother the noise inside my head, but there was nowhere to go.

So I sat. My palms sweated, my jaw clenched, and I let the storm run its course. The feelings rose like a tide, fierce, and choking, but eventually they began to ebb. For the first time, I discovered that emotions did not have to kill me if I stayed with them.

It was not a triumph. It was uncomfortable and lonely. But in that locked cell, I began to understand something I had never allowed before: sometimes survival is not about running—it is about staying still.

For most of my life, emotions had been enemies. Anxiety was a signal to find chemicals that would give me focus or numbness. Shame was a reason to hide or lash out. Grief was something to bury under noise, food, or another round of drinks. I thought I was escaping them, but in reality, I was building a prison tighter than steel bars.

In the closed prison cell, with nothing left to run to, I had no choice but to face them. At first, it felt unbearable. My old reflexes screamed for relief—the itch for amphetamines to straighten my thoughts, the fantasy of cocaine's brief rush, and even the memory of a fridge full of food. None of it was there. All I had was my body and the storm inside it.

Anxiety was the first visitor. It arrived as it always had: chest tight, jaw clenched, and breath shallow. Before, I would have silenced it with a line of speed, tricking myself into believing I was in control. Now I forced myself to sit still and simply observe the effect. My chest is tight, I told myself. My thoughts are racing. My body is bracing for a threat that is not here. Naming it did not erase the tension, but it shifted my relationship to it. Instead of being dragged around by panic, I could observe it like weather—something passing through me rather than something I had to fight.

Then came shame. I felt the heat climb into my cheeks, my gaze wanting to drop to the floor. In the past, I would have escaped by withdrawing—walking out of the room, reaching for a drink, or cracking a joke to deflect. But alone in the cell, there was no one to impress or hide from, so I stayed with the flush. I let my face burn and my stomach drop, and I realized the sensation itself was not lethal. Shame was painful, yes, but not fatal. It was just my nervous system's way of warning me I might lose connection. In that moment, I did not lose connection—I gained one with myself.

Grief came more slowly. For years, I had kept it buried under layers of substances and bravado. The losses—of my uncle, of friends, and of relationships I had wrecked—had been filed away in a locked cabinet. One night, as I sat on the edge of the bunk, those memories surfaced. My throat tightened, and a heaviness settled across my chest. I swallowed hard, my body bracing against the swell, reminding myself—I do not cry. Instead, I let the sorrow rise inside me like a tide pressing against the walls. I felt it fully—the ache, the emptiness, the weight of what had been taken. But for the first time, I did not drown it in alcohol, bury it under noise, or smother it with distractions. I let it move through me and then fade, like a wave breaking and pulling back. Grief had not destroyed me. It had passed.

What surprised me most was not how much these feelings hurt, but how much they changed once I stopped fighting them. When I finally let emotions pass through me, they lost some of their terror. Anxiety became a wave instead of drowning, shame became heat instead of exile, and grief became heaviness instead of silence.

I did not conquer them that night or in the weeks that followed. They still came, sometimes stronger than I thought I could bear. But every time I sat still and endured, I learned something vital: emotions were not executioners. They were signals, guides, even teachers. The more I faced them head-on, the less power they had to control me from the shadows.

In the end, the locked cell did not just confine me—it gave me the space to prove to myself that I could survive my own feelings. That discovery, as raw and painful as it was, became the foundation for everything that followed.

When I began to change on the inside, the effects rippled outward into my relationships. Transformation was never just about me sitting in a cell, facing shame or grief; it also depended on how I connected—or disconnected—from the people around me.

The Big Shifts

The first and most profound shift came with Riina. From the beginning, she was not impressed by chaos, bravado, or the masks I had worn for years. She did not need me to play the strongest man in the room or the loudest one at the table. What mattered was connection—the steady presence of a partner in life. That bond gave me something I had never experienced before: safety without conditions. Sitting beside her in silence felt more real than all the noise I once mistook for loyalty. Even her dog, Mr. Damien, leaning against my leg, seemed to test whether I could be steady enough to be trusted. The answer was not immediate, but the question stayed with me. Riina's presence—quiet, patient, and unwavering—showed me that partnership itself could be transformative.

Our wedding day.

The second shift came in my peer circles. For years, my environment was built on running—running from pain, from responsibility, even from silence. Those rooms, filled with laughter and chaos, once felt like belonging. But when I began the work of transformation, I saw that no half-measure would ever be enough. I could not reform myself while staying in the same environment. The old circles were magnets pulling me back into survival mode, no matter what insights I gained in solitude. So I made the hardest choice: I cut ties completely. I isolated myself from the circles that had once defined me. At first, it felt brutal, like cutting off parts of my own identity, but over time, I understood it was the only way a complete change could happen. Without altering the environment, the inner work would collapse under constant pressure.

The third shift was in how I spoke to myself. For most of my life, my inner voice was a punisher: idiot, failure, and weak. Shame dictated the script, and I believed it. But as I studied psychology, wrote in journals, and tested myself in the prison yard, I began experimenting with a different tone. Instead of, "You always blow it," I told myself, "This is shame—it will pass." Instead of "You're worthless," I tried, "You're learning." At first, the words felt foreign, as if I were lying to myself. But slowly, repetition carved new tracks. The critic softened into an observer, and the observer made space for growth.

Together, these shifts—bonding with Riina, cutting loose the old environment, and reshaping my inner dialogue—became the foundation of transformation. Facing emotions in solitude was one piece of the puzzle. Changing the relationships around me was the other. Without both, the old patterns would have swallowed me whole.

Transformation is often painted as a victory parade: you cut ties, you grow, and suddenly the world applauds. The truth is less glamorous. When I walked out of prison in 2017, the first and most decisive step was cutting off the old circles. I knew I could not change my life while staying in the same environment. That separation gave me space to breathe, but it also brought invisible costs and hidden wins.

The Win Comes with a Cost

The first cost was loneliness. Walking away from my old circles meant removing the noise, the reckless laughter, and the late-night chaos that had once passed for companionship. At first, the silence felt brutal. Nights stretched longer, and the absence of familiar voices left a void. Even when I was with new people, the temptation to fill the emptiness with alcohol or substances remained. Between 2017 and 2019, I still drank and used occasionally in entertainment settings. It was not daily chaos anymore—but it was not true freedom either.

The second cost was vulnerability. Facing emotions raw made me feel exposed. Anxiety rattled in my chest, shame flushed through my face, and grief pulled me under in waves. Before, I could drown all that in alcohol, amphetamines, or steroids. Now, stripped of the old circles and using far less, I was left with myself. That exposure was terrifying, as if every weakness I had spent years hiding were now staring me down in the mirror.

But the turning point came in February 2019. By then, the shit bucket had filled to the brim. I could no longer lie to myself that "occasional" use was harmless. I saw the patterns too clearly—the emptiness afterward, the cycle waiting to repeat. I decided, once and for all, to turn absolutist: no medication, no treatment program. Just a line I drew inside myself that I refused to cross again.

That decision revealed the hidden wins. Loneliness gave way to clarity. Vulnerability became strength. The absence of substances created space for trust—not in others, but in myself. For the first time, my self-esteem was not built on bravado, muscle, or chaos; it was built on sobriety, on the simple fact that I could face reality sober and still stand.

The costs were real—loneliness, exposure, temptation. But the wins were greater: clarity, trust, and resilience. Cutting off the old circles in 2017 opened the door. By going absolutist in February 2019, I finally stepped through it.

For most of my life, emotions were signals to run. Anxiety tightened my chest—reach for amphetamine. Shame flushed my face—drown it in alcohol. Grief surfaced—bury it in food or noise. Each avoidance reinforced the same loop: the amygdala, the brain's fear and alarm center, stayed hyperactive, primed to bolt at the first sign of discomfort.

When I stopped running—first partially after prison, then wholly in 2019—something different began to happen. Neuroscience calls it exposure with processing. Instead of masking the feeling, I let it rise, sit in my body, and pass through. Each time I did that, even for a few minutes, my brain was effectively retraining itself. The prefrontal cortex, the planning, and regulating part of the brain, had a chance to step in. Gradually, it learned: shame does not mean collapse, anxiety does not mean danger, grief does not mean annihilation.

Think of it like working with a skittish horse. If every time the horse flinches, you yank the reins and let it bolt, the fear circuit only strengthens. But if you stand firm, let the horse tremble, and wait until it calms, the animal learns a new script: stillness is safe. My brain was that horse. Each time I stayed present with a racing heart or a flushed face, I was teaching it to stand instead of bolting.

This process did not erase emotions. The amygdala still fires, the body still reacts. But repeated exposure and processing together rewires the balance: the prefrontal cortex gains authority, the alarm signals more quickly, and resilience builds. Over time, the same feelings that once drove me to substances became signals I could observe without obeying.

Neuroscience puts words to what I lived: stopping avoidance shrinks the power of fear. Facing emotions strengthens regulation. It is not about never flinching; it is about teaching the mind that flinching does not mean fleeing.

Stopping the run was far scarier than the running itself. Running had been familiar—a quick drink, a reckless night, or a loud distraction. It blurred the edges just enough to keep me moving. Standing still, on the other hand, meant facing everything I had buried: the heat of shame in my cheeks, the restless pulse of anxiety in my chest, and the heavy silence of grief.

Yet it was in that stillness where the real growth began. By cutting off the old circles after 2017, reducing the chaos, and finally going absolutist in February 2019, I had no escape routes left. The void was uncomfortable, even brutal at times, but it forced me into clarity. Emotions that once ruled me became signals I could name, study, and survive without drowning. Loneliness revealed its hidden win: the beginning of trust in myself. Vulnerability proved that I could hold pain without bolting.

That period of halting the run was not the end of the journey—it was the ground-clearing before construction. I had stripped away the old patterns, silenced the old noise, and started to look inward with honesty.

The next challenge was bigger: learning to act differently in the world and not just naming emotions or surviving without substances, but building from ground zero.

Because survival without running is one thing, but building a life worth living is another.

If I Could Talk to My Younger Self

Emotions Are Signals, Not Enemies

You thought emotions were enemies, but they were not. Anxiety, shame, and grief were not executioners; they were signals. Every time you drowned them in alcohol, amphetamines, steroids, or noise, you were not escaping—you were building a tighter prison inside yourself.

The Night You Faced the Storm

That night in the closed cell, when there was nowhere left to run, you finally learned this: emotions will not kill you if you sit with them. Anxiety is a wave, not drowning. Shame is heat, not exile. Grief is heaviness, not silence. None of them lasts forever.

Redefining Strength

You thought strength meant running faster, but real strength was in staying still. By sitting through the storm, you began to find connection—first with yourself and then with others.

The Power of Steady Connection

You thought loyalty came from chaos and noise, but real connection came later—with Riina. Her steady presence, her silence beside you, and her trust showed you that a partner in life can be transformative.

The Brutality of Cutting Ties

You thought you could half-change, keeping one foot in old circles, but you could not. Cutting ties in 2017 was brutal, but it opened the door. By February 2019, when the shit bucket overflowed, you drew the line: absolutist—no more running. That choice gave you clarity, trust, and real self-respect.

Survival Rewritten

You thought survival was about escaping, but survival was about learning to stand still, to face what came, and to build from ground zero.

The Truth About Growth

Because running only keeps you alive, stillness is where growth begins.

CHAPTER 8

Building from Ground Zero

A New Beginning: Education and Businesses

The envelope slid across the desk in the open prison, its thin weight belying the heaviness it carried. My name was written in neat block letters, beneath it the words: *Swedish level test course.* I was thirty-eight years old, sitting in a room that smelled faintly of disinfectant and dust, staring at a task most people had finished before they were old enough to vote.

The silence pressed in around me, broken only by the distant clink of keys on a guard's belt. I held the pen loosely, feeling its plastic ridges bite into my fingertips. The bars across the window cast long shadows across the page, sharp black lines against white paper–reminders of where I was, but also strange markers pointing forward, like a road drawn in reverse.

Shame rose first. Every word I struggled to translate felt like an indictment of wasted years. I thought about the time I had poured into chaos, into substances, into circles that led me nowhere. I imagined all the younger faces, already years ahead in their education and careers. For a moment, the pen felt heavier than I could lift.

But beneath the shame, something else stirred. Pride–not triumphant, not loud, but steady. The fact that I was even here, starting again at thirty-eight, mattered. The test was not just about Swedish. It was about proving that a man with scars and failures could start anew. The bars held me in, yes, but that day they also marked the first step toward breaking free.

When I enrolled in high school inside the open prison in 2017, it was not hesitation that defined me, but a decision. For years, my life had been marked by drifting–reacting, escaping, improvising. Going back to school at thirty-eight was the opposite of drifting. It was deliberate. I had looked at the wreckage behind me and decided: no more running.

High school was a practical step, but it carried symbolic weight. Most people completed it in their teens, moving seamlessly into work or further studies. I had bypassed that path long ago, convincing myself that chaos was my classroom and survival my diploma. But inside the prison, stripped of distractions, I saw clearly how wrong I had been. Education was not just about credentials; it was about reclaiming a part of myself I had abandoned.

The first course was Swedish–a level test that measured how much I remembered, how much I could still retrieve from the recesses of my mind. It was not easy. Years of substances, chaos, and instability had dulled my focus. Sitting down with pen and paper felt foreign, almost like handling fragile instruments after years of blunt tools. But there was also something unnerving about it. Each question demanded patience. Each answer, once completed, offered a flicker of progress.

Those early assignments became quiet victories. Not spectacular, not visible to anyone outside the prison walls, but profound in their impact. I began to rediscover patience–a quality survival mode had never allowed. Survival mode had trained me to act fast: fix the feeling, escape the pressure, silence the noise. Learning mode asked for something else entirely: sit with the problem, tolerate the discomfort, trust the process.

The contrast was stark. Survival mode burned through energy but left me empty. Learning mode, slow and methodical, left me tired but fuller, as if every effort had built a small layer of foundation. By the time I submitted the first assignments, a subtle shift had taken root. Education was no longer just an abstract idea; it was a lived experience, one that proved I was capable of building something beyond chaos.

Starting high school in prison was not a grand gesture; it was the simple act of beginning. But within that was a declaration: it is not too late to build, and not too late to change.

Remotely studying high school inside an open prison demanded a kind of discipline I had never practiced before. There were no classrooms, no bells, no teachers standing at the front reminding me of deadlines. What I had instead was silence, a desk, and the weight of responsibility resting entirely on my shoulders. At thirty-eight, I was both the student and the supervisor of my own progress.

The prison environment was paradoxical. On the one hand, it was restrictive—bars, routines, surveillance. On the other hand, it offered a kind of enforced stillness I had never known on the outside. That stillness became the space where I could focus. Remote learning required structure, and I had spent most of my life resisting it. Now it has become my lifeline.

Each course arrived in the form of materials, assignments, and deadlines that I had to manage myself. There were no excuses available. If I failed to complete an essay or missed a deadline, it was not because a teacher did not push me; it was because I had not shown up. That accountability was sobering. For years, I had deflected responsibility onto others, the system, and even bad luck. Remote study stripped away those escape hatches. If I wanted progress, I had to create it.

I began to carve out routines. Mornings were for study time, afternoons for assignments, and evenings for reviewing notes. It was not an invigorating activity; it was just repetition, day after day. But repetition was precisely what I had lacked in my earlier life. Where chaos once dictated my pace, now discipline did. Each completed assignment, no matter how small, became proof that consistency could build something solid.

The hardest part was sustaining focus. My mind, conditioned by years of quick fixes and restless searching, wanted constant stimulation. Remote study forced me to slow down, to wrestle with material that did not reward me instantly. At first, surprisingly, it was not exhausting to sit with a problem until it yielded an answer, even though, at that moment, it did not give me anything special. But over time, I began to feel a different kind of energy. It was not the rush of amphetamine or the false courage of alcohol. It was quieter, steadier: the satisfaction of persistence.

Remote learning also taught me the value of solitude. What once felt like punishment—being alone with my thoughts—became an asset. Without the noise of old circles or the chaos of my former lifestyle, I could hear myself think. Solitude became less of a cage and more of a workshop. In that space, I was not just completing assignments; I was rebuilding how I related to effort itself.

By the time I had completed the first full term, I realized something important: education was not about competing with younger students outside, nor about catching up to anyone else's timeline. It was about proving to myself that I could stay the course. Remote learning gave me exactly what survival never had—patience, consistency, and the ability to trust a process.

Somewhere along the way, studying stopped feeling like a sentence to serve and began to feel like an opening. At first, the textbooks were just tasks to get through, pages to turn so I could move forward. But gradually, something shifted. I noticed myself asking questions that were not on the assignment sheets. Why do people act the way they do? How do systems hold together? What is behind the rules we follow without thinking?

Curious Like a Child

For the first time since childhood, curiosity came alive in me. It was faint at first, almost fragile, but I could feel it growing with each subject I tackled. Mathematics, which I had once dismissed as tedious, became a quiet exercise in patience and order. Each equation was a puzzle with a solution waiting to be uncovered if I stuck with it long enough. Psychology opened a mirror, showing me that shame, anxiety, and grief were not personal failures but universal human experiences. History and civics gave me perspective, connecting my small story to broader currents of society.

Curiosity changed the way I read, wrote, and even thought. Instead of treating study as a chore, I began to approach it as a conversation—between me and the text, my past and my future. The same mind that once chased chaos now chased understanding. That shift felt more radical than any external change I had ever made.

In curiosity, I also found freedom. It was not the reckless freedom of running from responsibility, but the steadier freedom of choice. I could choose to explore, to learn, to grow. And in that freedom, I realized something vital: education was not only about earning a diploma. It was about reclaiming my right to wonder, to imagine, to build a mind that belonged entirely to me.

Rediscovering curiosity did not erase the years I had lost, but it transformed how I carried them. Where shame once lived, there was now a hunger to know more. Where fear once held me back, there was now a sense of possibility. In that quiet transformation, curiosity became not just a tool for learning; it became the first spark of a life rebuilt on purpose.

When I moved from a closed prison to an open prison in early 2017, education became more than a private project—it was something I carried with me as I prepared to re-enter the outside world. The transition was not simple. Freedom, even partial freedom, came with noise, temptations, and the old shadows of my past life. I knew the risks. Many before me had slipped back into old circles, old habits, old chaos.

But I had made a choice. Education was no longer just about passing time or earning credits—it was the anchor I needed to stay steady. While others in the open prison focused on counting days, I was counting assignments. My high school courses became the structure that kept me from drifting. Swedish lessons in the evenings, math problems in the mornings, essays scratched out in silence—they filled the hours with something that pointed forward instead of backward.

There were challenges, of course. Some nights, after long days of transition work, I stared at assignments with heavy eyes, wondering how I could keep up. There were moments when the old voices whispered: *This is pointless; you are too far behind.* But those whispers did not stick. Not anymore. Because I had already proven, back in the closed prison, that persistence mattered more than speed.

Balancing education with release meant learning discipline in a new way. Inside, the walls did part of the work for you. Outside, even in partial release, you had to create your own walls—boundaries to keep chaos at bay. I found those boundaries in the rhythm of study. Every finished course was proof that I could build, not just survive. Every credit earned was another brick in a foundation I had once believed was gone forever.

By the time I stepped fully into freedom, I was not walking out empty-handed. I carried books, assignments, and a growing belief that learning could protect me better than any armor I had built before. Education became the bridge between who I had been and who I was becoming—a bridge I walked every day, one page, one test, one lesson at a time.

By 2019, something I once thought impossible became reality: I finished high school, not as a teenager surrounded by classmates, but as a forty-year-old man who had carried textbooks through prison corridors and studied alone under harsh fluorescent lights. When the last assignments were turned in and the official papers confirmed it, I felt a quiet pride. It wasn't about the diploma itself— it was about proving that the years I thought were lost could still be reshaped into something meaningful.

But even before graduating, I had already widened the horizon. While completing high school courses, I enrolled in the Open University. I did not want to wait until one stage was over to begin the next; time was precious, and I had wasted enough of it in the past. Juggling the basics of high school with the challenges of university-level studies demanded discipline I did not know I had. It was as if my mind, once dulled by substances and chaos, was finally awake and hungry.

After high school, I stepped directly into the University of Eastern Finland. There was no pause. No gap year. No drifting. Just forward motion. I chose administrative sciences, a field that felt both practical and expansive, giving me tools I could apply in real life as well as frameworks for thinking differently about law, systems, and society.

There was pride, yes, but also humility. Sitting with coursework in my late thirties, I knew most of my peers were a decade or more younger, already moving through the system I was just entering. But that thought did not sting. Instead, it gave me fuel. I had something many of them did not: a deep knowledge of what happens when you waste opportunity. For me, every lecture, every book, every passed exam was a refusal to go back.

My Graduation was not a loud celebration. It was quiet, like much of my journey. But in that quiet, I knew: the boy who once thought books were enemies had become a man who saw them as lifelines. And from here, the real climb was only beginning.

University Years

Stepping into the University of Eastern Finland in 2019 marked another turning point. High school had been about recovery—reclaiming ground I had lost, proving to myself that I could still learn. University, however, was about building. It was no longer about catching up; it was about moving forward with intent.

I chose administrative sciences, majoring in civil law. To many, that might sound like a dry field, but for me, it was alive with meaning. Every page I read connected directly to questions I had already lived: What holds societies together? How do rules and systems balance fairness and order? What happens when trust in institutions breaks down? These were not just academic theories. They were mirrors reflecting my own life and the world I had seen both inside and outside prison walls.

At first, the workload was daunting. Legal texts, complex frameworks, and the pace of higher education required focus, which I had not always been known for. But here was the difference: this time, I had purpose. I was no longer trying to survive the next hour or the next day. Each course I completed, each essay I turned in, became a building block toward a future I was consciously shaping.

Graduating with a bachelor's degree in 2021 was another quiet milestone. For someone else, it might have been just a step on a linear path. For me, it was a declaration that detours no longer defined my life. A year later, I completed my Master's in Administrative Science with a major in civil law. Those years gave me more than academic knowledge. They gave me a framework for thinking, a discipline for approaching problems, and confidence that I could stand on equal ground with anyone in my field.

University was not just about the classroom, though. It was about testing myself in an environment that demanded long-term commitment. It required consistency, patience, and humility—qualities I had once avoided but now found to be the foundation of progress.

Looking back, 2019 to 2022 was not just a stretch of study. It was a training ground, a proving ground, and a launchpad. With those degrees in my hand, I carried more than qualifications. I had proof that reinvention was not only possible—it was real.

Stepping Up Further

If the University of Eastern Finland had been about reclaiming and rebuilding, then King's College London was about stepping onto a wider stage. In 2023, when I began my Master of Laws in International Corporate and Commercial Law, I carried not only a degree but also the weight of everything it had taken to reach that point.

Walking into King's—even virtually at times, even from across borders—was a moment that symbolized more than academic ambition. It was proof that my journey had carried me from a prison cell with a Swedish test to one of the world's most respected law schools. The name alone carried gravity, but it was the environment that reshaped me. I was now surrounded by international peers, legal professionals, and professors who expected precision, discipline, and legal depth.

The coursework itself was demanding. Corporate structures, cross-border contracts, commercial disputes—every subject was layered with complexity. But unlike earlier years, I no longer questioned whether I belonged. The foundation I had built in Finland gave me the confidence to meet the challenge head-on. Late nights were no longer driven by desperation but by determination to master law at the highest level.

What King's gave me was not only another diploma but a professional transformation. Here, I was not just a student, nor an entrepreneur expanding his knowledge. I became a lawyer—not one rooted in national frameworks alone, but one with international competence, able to understand and operate within global legal systems.

Graduating in 2025 with a Master of Laws was more than an academic achievement. It was a declaration that my past did not define the limits of my future, and that I could stand as a legal professional with international reach.

King's is giving me more than a degree. It gave me a vantage point–proof that past detours do not limit transformation, and that the same discipline forged in solitude could carry me into the most demanding environments in the world.

Education gave me knowledge, but business gave me the chance to test that knowledge in the real world. By the time I founded my first company in 2018, even before finishing high school, I knew that entrepreneurship would be my laboratory. The firm began with consulting, and after I moved to open-university, I expanded into bookkeeping and legal and tax services, immediately applying my growing knowledge into practice. Modest on the surface, it was a place where I could practise the theories I was studying in real time. University was sharpening my mind; the company was sharpening my instincts.

Each year added another layer. In 2020, a second company came, then another in 2021, and a fourth in 2022. Each venture widened my reach, from construction to personnel services to property investment. But the greatest transformation came when I began operating internationally.

Uzbekistan became a defining chapter. I had not yet finished King's College at that time, but the seeds of international competence were already taking root. I was invited to an international conference where I spoke about law, labour, and entrepreneurship in a room filled with leaders and decision-makers. Soon after, I found myself in front of cameras, broadcast to tens of millions of viewers across the region. For someone who once struggled to believe he had a voice worth hearing, this was both surreal and affirming.

The trip showed me that credibility is not measured only by degrees completed, but also by the courage to step forward when opportunities present themselves. The experience in Uzbekistan strengthened my determination to finish my studies at King's. It gave me living proof that what I was building had global resonance.

Business gave me something education alone could not: scale. It tested whether my discipline could hold under pressure, whether my vision could expand beyond myself, and whether my story could inspire not just survival but contribution. Being a CEO, entrepreneur, lawyer, and investor is not only about profit margins—it is about impact and proof that resilience can evolve into leadership.

Looking back, the businesses were not just companies; they were extensions of the new identity I had fought to build. From a desk in open prison to global negotiations, from textbooks to television screens, each step reinforced the same truth: survival had become strategy, and strategy had become creation.

If I Could Talk to My Younger Self

The Desk That Changes Everything

You don't know it yet, but the moment you sit at that desk in prison with the psychological book in front of you will change your life. You'll feel shame first—the kind that whispers about lost years, missed chances, wasted time. But listen closely: beneath that shame, pride will begin to stir. The fact that you're even starting at thirty-eight will matter more than you can imagine.

Education Is About Direction, Not Age

Understand this: education is not about age, it's about direction. High school won't make you younger, but it will give you something far more valuable: momentum. For years, you drifted, surviving one crisis at a time. Picking up that pen will be the first deliberate step toward building instead of running.

The Silence Becomes Your Workshop

The silence will feel brutal at first. Remote study will mean no classrooms, no teachers hovering over you, just you against the page. But that silence will turn into your workshop. Day after day, assignment after assignment, you'll prove to yourself that consistency can rebuild what chaos tore apart.

The Return of Curiosity

Then something even more powerful will happen: curiosity will return. Math will teach you patience where chaos once demanded speed. Psychology will give you words for shame, anxiety, and grief, transforming enemies into signals. Law will open a window into systems that once crushed you—and show you how they can be navigated, even mastered.

Milestones of Education

Each degree will become a milestone: high school in 2019, Bachelor's in 2021, Master's in Finland in 2022, and King's College London in 2025. Remember this: you won't just be a lawyer. You'll be someone who can stand on any stage and know you belong there.

Business As the Laboratory

Business will be your laboratory. The companies you start—in 2018, 2020, 2021, and 2022—will test whether you can turn theory into practice. And they will. Your decisions will echo far beyond Finland. In Uzbekistan, you'll stand in front of leaders, you'll speak at a conference, and your words will reach tens of millions of people on TV. The same voice you once drowned in alcohol will travel across borders.

Transformation Through Subtraction

But know this, too: transformation won't come from addition, but subtraction. Cutting yourself off from the old circles will want to tear pieces of your identity away. It will hurt. It will be lonely. Yet loneliness will give you clarity, and clarity will give you strength.

The Absolutist Line

The turning point will come in February 2019. You'll see the cycle clearly, and you'll draw a line inside yourself that no one else can erase. No medication, no programs—just you deciding to go absolutist. That will be your greatest diploma. That will be the foundation of self-trust.

The Bars as Markers

Here's the truth I need you to carry: the bars that hold you in today are not only barriers—they are markers, pointing forward. They will remind you of where you've been, but also of what lies ahead if you keep choosing discipline over drift.

Freedom Beyond Prison

You are not too late. You are not too broken. You are not finished. The man you are becoming is built in silence, in patience, in persistence. And when you walk free, it won't just be freedom from prison—it will be freedom from the prison you carried inside yourself for far too long.

Learning to Dream Again

The prison was quiet, the kind of silence that presses against your ears. Outside my window, the bars cast their long shadows across the desk, the same desk where textbooks, notebooks, and loose sheets of paper lay in uneven piles. Some were high school assignments, others were books from different areas, such as philosophy, and in between them sat a worn notebook where I had begun sketching something new—not just answers for teachers but outlines for business plans.

It was late, the fluorescent light above humming faintly, my eyes sore from hours of reading. Years earlier, nights like this would have ended in a haze of alcohol, loud distractions, or another round of chaos. Now, instead of numbing myself, I was teaching myself to see. The numbers I scribbled were not just math problems; they were budgets. The case studies were not just lessons; they were blueprints for what I might build.

I felt the weight of lost time—nearly forty, sitting in a prison cell, studying high school while others my age were deep into careers. Shame flickered, sharp and familiar. But alongside it came something else: vision. For the first time, I wasn't thinking only about surviving the next day. I was imagining years ahead, imagining companies, imagining a life where strategy replaced reaction.

That night, surrounded by books and plans, I realized the cell no longer defined me. It contained me, yes—but inside it, something larger was being born: the ability to envision.

For most of my life, my thinking had been short-term—not by choice, but by necessity. Survival mode doesn't care about five years from now. It cares about the next ten minutes, the next hit, the next escape. If shame burned too hot, I drowned it. If anxiety rattled too loud, I silenced it. My mind was wired for immediate relief, not for patient planning.

That began to change when I sat with books and business ideas inside prison. At first, studying high school courses was simply about passing time—a way to keep my thoughts from spiralling. But as I worked through assignments, I noticed something: every subject was a lesson in patience. Math problems forced me to slow down, step by step. Psychology gave me language for my emotions. Each small completion showed me that progress came not from rushing, but from returning, again and again.

Around the same time, I began sketching out my first business ideas. The plans were simple at first—consultation services. But even those rough outlines taught me something survival never had: the value of thinking beyond today. A business wasn't built in a single night; it demanded foresight, structure, and vision. Just like high school, it was a long game.

The contrast was sharp. Short-term fixes had always left me empty. But long-term effort—finishing an essay, structuring a business plan, mapping out steps I couldn't yet take—gave me something new: direction. The future stopped being a vague threat and started becoming a place I could design.

The shift from survival to vision didn't happen in one leap. It happened in these quiet, deliberate acts—study, plan, repeat. And each choice proved I was capable of more than surviving. I was capable of building.

Survival mode is not just a mindset—it is a brain state. When life is lived moment to moment, the amygdala, our brain's alarm system, dominates. It floods the body with stress hormones, keeping us on high alert for threats. In that state, the prefrontal cortex—the part of the brain responsible for planning, problem-solving, and long-term thinking—goes partly offline. That is why survival feels so consuming: the brain is wired to focus on the immediate, not the future.

When I began studying in prison, something shifted on a neurological level. Each time I sat with a math problem or drafted an essay, I was training my prefrontal cortex to re-engage. The very act of focusing on structured work—breaking problems into steps, tolerating discomfort, delaying gratification—built new neural pathways. Instead of defaulting to "escape now," my brain was practicing "plan, persist, complete."

Business planning amplified this process. Sketching out even the simplest ideas—services, clients, timelines—forced me to think in months and years, not minutes and hours. Neuroscience shows that long-term visualization strengthens the brain's default mode network, the system that integrates memory, imagination, and identity. By drafting business plans, I was literally rehearsing a future self. My brain was learning to prefer steady, purpose-driven dopamine rewards—the satisfaction of progress—over the chaos-driven highs of substances.

The analogy is simple: survival mode is like sprinting on a treadmill—exhausting, repetitive, and going nowhere. Vision mode is like charting a hike up a mountain. The climb is harder and slower, but every step changes the view.

Neuroscience confirms what I felt: the shift from survival to vision is not just psychological. It is physical, cellular, and real. Each time I chose to study, to plan, to persist, I was rewiring my brain to stop bracing for disaster and start building for the future.

In education and business, I found a different kind of confidence—one rooted in evidence rather than illusion. Every completed course was proof that I could follow through. Every assignment returned with a passing grade was a fact that no one could take away. Each business I founded, no matter how small, carried the same message: you can create, not just consume; you can build, not just destroy.

This confidence was quieter than bravado, but far stronger. It did not need to shout or flex. It simply existed, anchored in honest work and real results. When doubts came—and they did—I could look at what I had already achieved and remind myself: this is not theory, this is fact.

Self-esteem, I realized, was not about pretending to be unshakable. It was about stacking small, steady proofs until belief became natural. For the first time, I did not have to perform strength; I could embody it. And that shift—from bravado to earned confidence—became one of the most liberating changes of my life.

A Declaration to Dream Again

When I walked into King's College London in 2023, it was more than enrolment. It was a declaration. From the outside, it looked like another step on an academic journey. However, to me, it was the clearest symbol yet that dreams, no matter how delayed, could still be claimed.

King's represented possibility on a scale I once thought forever closed to me. Years earlier, I had sat in a prison cell wrestling with high school assignments. Now, I was part of one of the most prestigious law schools in the world, surrounded by students and professors from every corner of the globe. Their presence reminded me that law was not only national, but international—a shared language that could shape borders, contracts, and futures. And for the first time, I felt I belonged in that conversation.

Belonging was the real breakthrough. For much of my life, I had felt like an outsider, marked by detours and scars. At King's, the focus was not on where you came from but on what you could contribute. Each lecture, each case study, each late night of study was a reminder that I was not behind–I was exactly where I needed to be.

Education had become more than a ladder; it was a window into possibility. King's College gave me not only knowledge but a new vantage point. It proved that rebuilding was not just about survival or catching up–it was about stepping into spaces I had once only dared to dream of and discovering that I could belong there fully.

If education gave me knowledge, entrepreneurship gave me identity. For most of my earlier life, I had been known for what I broke–rules, relationships, even myself. Founding my first company while still finishing high school marked a turning point: for the first time, I was building something rather than tearing it down.

The business started modestly, yet even those small beginnings carried weight. Each client I served, and each contract I handled, was a reminder that I was capable of creation, not just survival. The work gave structure to my days, proof that discipline was not only for assignments and exams but could generate value in the real world.

From there, the momentum grew. A second company in 2020, a third in 2021, a fourth in 2022–each venture widened my reach, from construction and staffing to property investment. These businesses were not only about income; they were laboratories where I tested the very skills education had sharpened, like patience, structure, and problem-solving. They became proof that I could step into the marketplace not as a consumer of chaos, but as a builder of order.

Identity Shift

What mattered most was the identity shift. With every business registered and every risk taken, I moved further away from the man who had once relied on substances and bravado for confidence. Now, my self-esteem comes from tangible results: jobs created, agreements signed, and goals met.

Entrepreneurship planted the seeds of both financial independence and impact. It showed me that freedom was not just the absence of prison walls or old habits, but the ability to shape reality with my own vision. In building businesses, I was also rebuilding myself—not as a destroyer, but as a builder of futures.

Entrepreneurship did not stay local for long. The skills I was sharpening through education and business soon opened doors that stretched far beyond Finland. One of the most pivotal moments came in Uzbekistan.

I was invited to speak at an international conference, sharing insights on law, labour, and entrepreneurship. The room was filled with leaders, policymakers, and decision-makers—people I never imagined I would stand alongside. Soon after, I found myself on television, my words broadcast to tens of millions across the region.

I rented a helicopter during one of my trips to Uzbekistan.

View from the helicopter.

A happy HELO passenger.

At that moment, I realized how far I had come. Not long before, I had been locked in a cell, struggling through high school assignments. Now, I was contributing to international dialogue, negotiating with governments, and demonstrating through action that resilience can become leadership.

I had not yet completed my Master of Laws at King's College, but standing there proved something: credibility is not only built by diplomas, but also by courage, persistence, and the willingness to step forward.

That leap beyond borders showed me that my story—once confined by walls—had grown into something with global reach. Education gave me tools, entrepreneurship gave me practice, and together they gave me a platform that stretched further than I had ever dared to dream.

For much of my life, hope had felt like a dangerous thing. To hope meant to imagine something better, and too often those hopes collapsed under the weight of reality—broken promises, failed attempts, or the chaos I created myself. Hope felt like a setup for disappointment, so I learned to replace it with action, distraction, or denial.

But as education and entrepreneurship began to take root, something changed. Hope was no longer a fragile dream floating in the distance. It became something I could anchor in action and proof. Every completed assignment, every credit earned, every course passed gave me evidence that progress was possible. Each business I built showed me that I could create, not just destroy. The results might have been modest at first, but they were real, tangible markers that I could point to when doubt tried to creep in.

That shift transformed how I carried myself. Hope was no longer a liability; it was a resource. It fuelled late nights of study and long hours of planning, not with empty fantasy but with grounded belief. The kind of hope I found was not about waiting for life to change—it was about knowing that with work, discipline, and persistence, I could change it myself.

For the first time, hope was not something to fear. It was something to build on.

For years, I had carried the identity of a lone wolf. It felt safer to depend on no one, to keep my guard up, and to let distance shield me from disappointment. Survival had taught me that trust was a liability. But as my life began to shift, so did the role of relationships.

Riina became the grounding force—a steady partnership that reflected both my progress and my struggles. With her, silence was not emptiness; it was safety. Even the smallest gestures—her patience, her presence, her trust—reminded me that I did not have to carry everything alone.

That partnership reshaped my sense of self. I was no longer just a survivor, moving through life in isolation. I was a partner, someone who could share responsibility, build alongside another, and dream beyond my own limitations. The shift rippled outward, into how I led in business and how I carried myself in the world.

Through her, I learned that strength does not diminish when shared. It grows—turning a lone wolf into a partner, a leader, and ultimately, a dreamer.

In prison, the bars once felt like finality—cold markers of endings. But over time, I began to see them differently: not just boundaries, but lines pointing forward, marking the possibility of new beginnings. That shift stayed with me long after release.

For most of my life, my horizon ended at the next fix, the next night, the next escape. Tomorrow was a gamble, and legacy was a word for other people. But when I began to study, build businesses, and step onto international stages, the question changed: What will remain when I'm gone?

Legacy, for me, is not about children or bloodlines. It is about impact. It is about proving that resilience can turn into contribution, that scars can be repurposed as blueprints. Every company founded, every agreement signed, every talk given is more than an achievement—it is a seed planted.

The shift from "survive today" to "leave something behind" transformed how I live. Legacy is no longer abstract. It begins each time I choose to build rather than destroy.

There was a time when the word dream felt dangerous. Dreams meant disappointment, reminders of what I could not reach. But education, business, and the slow rebuilding of self-esteem changed that. Piece by piece, I learned that dreams did not have to stay abstract. They could be tested, structured, and pursued. They could become strategies.

Through all of this, hope stopped being fragile. It became anchored in work, consistency, and action. Every achievement, no matter how small, was a reminder that my past no longer dictated my future.

And yet, this was still only a beginning. Education gave me tools. Business gave me a platform. Relationships gave me grounding. But the next question was bigger: now that I had stopped running, now that I had begun to dream and to build, what kind of world did I want to create?

That question leads into the next chapter—a shift not just from surviving or rebuilding, but from creating a life that leaves a mark.

If I Could Talk to My Younger Self

Bars as Markers, Not Just Barriers

The bars you see now aren't only barriers—they're markers pointing forward. That desk with its piles of textbooks and scribbled business plans may feel small, but it's the place where you stop surviving and start building.

Survival Mode Is a Treadmill

You'll learn that survival mode—chasing the next hit, drowning shame, silencing grief—is just sprinting on a treadmill. Exhausting, repetitive, going nowhere. But when you sit still, study, and sketch plans, your brain begins to rewire itself. Step by step, you'll train it to think beyond today, to design a future instead of fearing it.

Real Confidence Comes from Evidence

Confidence won't come from bravado, substances, or muscle. It will come from evidence: one finished course, one passed exam, one client served. That kind of confidence is quieter but unshakable.

Dreams Don't Die—They Evolve

King's College, the companies you'll find, even standing on international stages—those things will prove that dreams don't die. They evolve. They become strategies.

From Survival to Building

And when hope comes back—not fragile this time but anchored in proof—you'll see that you're no longer just surviving. You're building.

Strength Shared, Circles Cut

Riina will show you that strength grows when shared. Cutting off old circles will prove that isolation is sometimes the only doorway to transformation. And contribution—to others, to systems, to the world—will rewire you more deeply than survival ever could.

Redefining Legacy

Legacy won't mean children. It will mean impact. Proof that scars can become blueprints.

Becoming in the Stillness

So, hold on. Don't run. Sit with the storm. Because in those quiet nights, with books and plans under prison light, you are not just enduring. You are becoming.

CHAPTER 9

From Surviving to Creating

How Contribution Rewired My Brain

The room was heavy with anticipation. Rows of faces stretched before me—leaders, policymakers, business figures—their eyes fixed on the stage. A microphone stood inches from my mouth, its cool metal catching the light. The glare of spotlights blurred the edges of the hall, but I could feel the silence settling, waiting for me to speak.

For a heartbeat, I sat still, feeling the weight of the moment. Years ago, silence like this would have terrified me—the empty pause before chaos, the space where my own mind turned against me. Back then, I was a man who couldn't even control his own thoughts, let alone shape anything beyond the reach of a single night. Substances, bravado, and noise had been my only tools.

But now, in that silence, I carried something different: structure, clarity, vision. I wasn't just speaking for myself. I was representing ideas that could move workers across borders, and the possibility of building systems where others once saw only barriers.

When I leaned into the microphone, my voice felt steady—not because I had erased the chaos of my past, but because I had transformed it into purpose. Each word carried the contrast: the man who once ran from emotions now stood, anchoring policies and influencing futures.

The lights were hot, the hall was vast, but in that moment, I wasn't small anymore. I was part of something larger. The silence broke into applause, and I realized: contribution had rewired me as deeply as survival once had.

Survival mode is narrow. When you're trapped inside it, the brain reduces everything to a single, urgent question: what do I need right now? The amygdala, the brain's alarm system, dominates. Its job is to keep you alive, not to help you grow. That is why survival feels so consuming. It tunnels your vision into the next ten minutes—the next hit, next escape, and next distraction. Sobriety quieted that cycle, but on its own, it wasn't enough. What truly began rewiring me was contribution.

Contribution forces the brain to expand. The moment you stop asking only how I get through this day and begin asking how I impact others, you activate different systems. Neuroscience shows that empathy circuits and the prefrontal cortex light up when we plan not just for ourselves, but for people around us. In practice, which means the same brain that once calculated the fastest way to numb pain now calculates how to build structures, solve problems, and meet needs bigger than your own.

Me and Mr Reddington.

Our newcomer, Ms Prada.

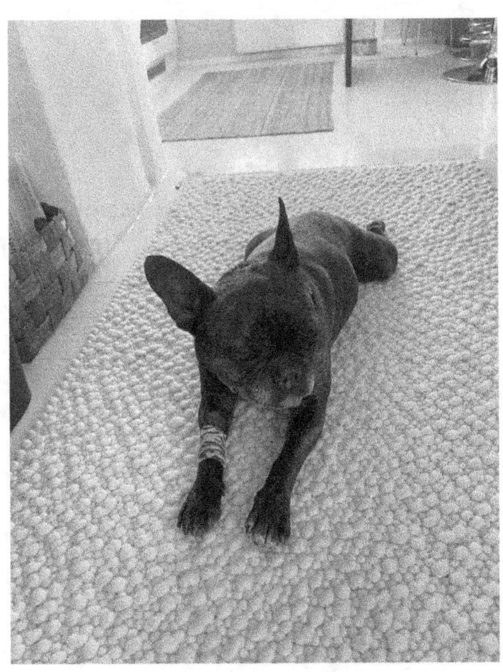

Mrs Pulla, aka Grandma.

For me, this shift started small—business plans drafted between high school assignments, notes scratched in a worn notebook. At first, they were small business ideas. But even those modest outlines stretched my thinking beyond survival. Suddenly, it wasn't just about me. It was about clients, contracts, and outcomes that affected more than one life. My brain was rehearsing a new identity: not just a survivor, but a contributor.

The real transformation came when the contribution reached a higher level, like an international stage or a domestic audience. Standing at conferences, negotiating agreements, or even speaking into a television camera —those moments demanded that I think outward. What do they need to understand? How do my words shape trust, opportunity, or direction? It wasn't performance; it was responsibility. Responsibility recruits different neural pathways. The dopamine that once spiked from chaos-driven highs now came from purpose-driven action—from seeing results ripple into other lives.

Contribution built resilience in a way that sobriety alone never could. Sobriety taught me to face my own storms without escape. Contribution taught me to stand steady for others, even when storms still rumbled inside me. It required me to regulate not only my emotions, but also my decisions, because the consequences no longer ended with me. When others depended on my consistency—employees, clients, partners—I had to strengthen the very circuits that survival mode had left weak: planning, patience, empathy, and foresight.

Neuroscience confirms what I lived: when you shift from self-preservation to contribution, your brain literally expands its map. The prefrontal cortex integrates memory and vision, the empathy networks strengthen connections, and the default mode network begins weaving a future where you are not the only center. That rewiring is resilience in its truest form—not just the ability to withstand your own chaos, but the capacity to build order for others. Contribution was more than action. It was medicine for the mind—the proof that healing deepens when your purpose reaches beyond yourself.

For most of my life, I had been known for what I broke. I broke the rules. At the beginning of my journey, I also broke trust, and in the process, broke myself. Destruction had been my default mode; chaos left in my wake. So, when I founded my first company while still studying, the act itself was radical. It wasn't about the size of the business or the profit margins; it was about proving to myself that I could build something instead of tearing it down.

That first venture wasn't much, but to me, it was everything. It gave me a structure to test the knowledge I was gathering at the Open University and, later, at the University of Eastern Finland. Each client I advised, each contract I reviewed, and each number I balanced was proof that my effort could produce order—order where there had once been only chaos.

The pattern repeated itself in the years that followed. Each venture grew out of the last, branching into construction, staffing, property investment, and beyond. Every registration form I filed and every business I launched was more than an administrative task; it was a declaration. The man who once burned time and opportunity was now generating value, not only for himself but for others.

What surprised me most about entrepreneurship wasn't the work itself, but the responsibility it demanded. When you hire someone or build a team, their livelihoods become intertwined with your consistency. That reality hit me with a weight heavier than any prison bar. In the past, my recklessness had hurt me most of all. But now, recklessness wasn't an option. My decisions determined not just whether I thrived, but whether others could pay their rent, support their families, or feel secure in their work.

Leadership became a new classroom. Textbooks had sharpened my mind, but entrepreneurship tested my character. Leading meant balancing empathy with firmness, vision with patience. It meant learning to listen when my instinct was to push and learning to push when my instinct was to hesitate. It demanded a level of stability I had never practiced before–the kind that turns chaos into clarity.

Each business became a reflection of this transformation. Consulting showed me the power of expertise. Staffing revealed the responsibility of matching people with opportunities. Construction taught me about structure, timelines, and patience. Property investment forced me to think long-term, to weigh risks and rewards not in days but in years. In every field, the common thread was the same: building.

Entrepreneurship also rewired my relationship with confidence. Before, bravado had been my mask–loud, inflated, temporary. Now, confidence came quietly from results that could not be faked–a contract signed. A project delivered. A paycheck issued. These were tangible proofs that discipline, once my enemy, had become my ally. The muscles I once built in gyms with steroids now existed in my businesses: strength forged not by chemicals, but by consistency.

Looking back at those years, I see more than companies; I see a record of transformation. Each business was an anchor, pulling me further away from the man I had been and closer to the one I was becoming. They were living proof that destruction no longer defined me. Creation did.

Entrepreneurship wasn't just about financial independence. It was about identity. It showed me that I could hold responsibility without collapsing, that I could create order where once I only left wreckage, and that I could lead others with the steadiness I had once searched for in myself.

In building those companies, I wasn't just shaping businesses; I was shaping a new self–a builder, not a destroyer.

Chaos into Clarity

The air in the conference hall in Uzbekistan carried a weight I could feel even before I stepped onto the stage. Rows of delegates sat waiting, their suits crisp, eyes focused, and notebooks open. Above me, the lights were hot, and in front of me, a microphone stood—a thin line between silence and influence. I had spoken in rooms before—to friends, to judges, to people who doubted me—but this was different. Here, my words were not just filling space; they were shaping perceptions, building bridges, and perhaps shifting possibilities for thousands of people I would never meet.

When I began to speak, the room quieted in a way that was both unnerving and powerful. I talked about law, labor, societies, and collaboration—topics that were once distant abstractions but had become real through my work and studies. I spoke not only from theory, but from lived experience. My voice, steady yet deliberate, carried across the hall, translated in real time for those who did not share my language. For the first time in my life, the chaos that once defined me had been transformed into clarity—into words that people leaned in to hear.

Then came the television appearance. Sitting in a studio, lights glaring, cameras trained directly on me, I felt the strangeness of scale. Years earlier, my words had influenced only a handful of people in a smoky flat, a prison cell, or a circle built on noise and recklessness. Now, I was speaking to tens of millions across a region, my face and voice broadcast far beyond anything I could see. The gravity of that moment pressed against me like an invisible weight.

Contribution changed me in those moments, and not only in obvious ways. It humbled me first. Standing before leaders, policymakers, and millions of unseen viewers, I understood how small I really was. My story—my voice—was only one among billions. I was not the center of the world, not even close. But at the same time, it expanded me. Knowing that something I said could ripple outward, influence decisions, or inspire possibility in someone I would never meet gave me a sense of connection far larger than myself.

That paradox—being smaller and larger at the same time—became the heart of transformation through contribution. Humility kept me grounded; expansion gave me purpose. Together, they replaced the old, destructive illusion of power. When I was younger, I believed that control came from volume, from force, from being the loudest or strongest in a room. But true influence, I discovered, came from clarity and substance—from showing that scars can become blueprints.

The agreements I signed in Uzbekistan, including those with government officials on labor supply, carried that same weight. They were not just business contracts; they were commitments that could impact communities, workers, and families. For someone who had once been unable to manage his own chaos, being responsible for shaping structures that touched the lives of others was almost overwhelming. It was as though I was being tested: Could I hold this responsibility? Could I channel it into something that builds rather than destroys?

The answer, I discovered, was yes. Not because I was flawless, but because I had already faced myself in silence, in prison cells, and in study halls. The discipline forged there had prepared me for the responsibility of influence. Contribution was no longer abstract; it was tangible, measurable, and humbling.

Looking back, those moments in Uzbekistan became more than memories. They were markers of a shift: from a man who once believed his actions affected no one but himself to a man who knew his words, decisions, and commitments could ripple across borders. Contribution transformed me not just by what I gave, but by what it revealed—that my life had grown larger than my own survival.

Contribution did not just change what I was doing—it changed how my brain was wired. For years, my nervous system had been tuned to one frequency: escape. Every decision was filtered through survival–how do I get through this hour, this night, this feeling? That wiring kept me alive, but it also kept me trapped.

When I began to contribute–through education, business, and international agreements and platforms–something shifted. My focus was no longer only inward, consumed by what I lacked or feared. It turned outward. I found myself thinking about employees, partners, and communities. The same energy that had once been spent running from pain was now being channeled into building something that could outlast me.

On a neurological level, it felt as if my brain were expanding. Planning was no longer about escaping consequences; it was about anticipating opportunities. Effort was not about numbing discomfort; it was about creating value. Even the dopamine rewards changed–not the short-lived rush of substances, but the deeper satisfaction of impact.

But contribution alone was not the whole story. Yes, it rewired me, giving me resilience and purpose that sobriety alone could not. Yet behind every deal signed, lecture given, and company built, there remained a shadow: the pain that had shaped me.

The next step was not only to contribute, but also to confront that pain and ask the harder question: What if the very wounds I carried could become part of the purpose I offered the world?

If I Could Talk to My Younger Self

Escape Mode and Survival Wiring

You've been living in escape mode for so long that you don't even realize it's wiring your brain to think only about survival. Every decision feels like it's about the next hour, the next hit, the next way to get out of pain. That's not weakness–that's your nervous system doing its job. But here's what I need you to know: survival is not the whole story.

From Survival to Contribution

One day, you'll discover something different. When you stop running and start contributing, your brain will begin to change. Instead of asking, "How do I get through this night?" you'll find yourself asking, "How do I build something that lasts?" Instead of fighting only for your own relief, you'll feel responsible for others—for your team, for your partners, and for the people who depend on what you create. That responsibility won't crush you. It will expand you.

Purpose Replaces the Rush

The rush you once chased in substances will be replaced by something stronger—the quiet satisfaction of impact. The sense of emptiness will give way to purpose. You'll realize that planning, effort, and patience aren't punishments. They're tools that let you shape reality.

Pain as Fuel for Purpose

Here's the most important part: contribution is not the end of the journey. Behind the companies, the agreements, the speeches, the shadow of pain will still be there. Don't be afraid of it. That pain isn't just baggage—it's raw material. And if you let it, it will become the very fuel for your purpose.

Turning Pain into Purpose

The night was still, broken only by the scratch of my pen against paper. A single lamp lit the desk, the rest of the room heavy with shadow. The journal lay open, blank lines daring me to fill them. For years, nights like this had been drowned in alcohol, blurred in chaos, or numbed by substances. Now there was no noise, no escape—only me, my memories, and the silence I had once feared.

The memories came hard: faces I had lost, choices that had burned bridges, and the chaos I had built with my own hands. Shame pressed on me; grief weighed me down. But instead of burying it, I wrote it. Line after line, the pain poured out—raw, messy, unfiltered.

Then something shifted. The words on the page no longer looked like weapons aimed at me; they looked like lessons. The very scars I had spent years hiding began to take shape as stories. Wounds became warnings. Failures became proof. What had once almost destroyed me could now be repurposed.

That night, I realized I wasn't just writing for myself; I was building fuel. The journal was not a dumping ground—it was a forge. Every sentence hammered the pain into something stronger—something I could use: to speak, to consult, to lead.

I had run from my past for so long, but here it was, becoming the very thing that would drive my future. Pain was no longer just suffering. It was material; it was a purpose.

For a long time, I treated my scars like secrets. Every mistake, every relapse, every night lost to chaos felt like a mark against me. I thought if people saw the truth—the shame, the psychosis, the grief—they would turn away. So I buried it, put on masks, and tried to project strength while hiding the cracks. What I didn't realize then was that the very scars I feared were the ones that would open doors.

When I began speaking openly, something shifted. I stopped polishing my story and started telling it raw. The shame I once thought would destroy me became the bridge to connect with others. People leaned in, not away, because they saw themselves in my struggle. The nights I had spent locked in with anxiety, the years I had tried to bury grief, even the clarity of realizing I was in psychosis—all of it gave me a language that textbooks alone could never provide.

Failure, I discovered, becomes credibility when you survive it. Anyone can talk about success, but not everyone can explain what it feels like to hit rock bottom and still crawl back up. My scars gave weight to my words. They weren't abstract theories—they were lived proof. When I said change was possible, it wasn't a motivational slogan; it was a fact, written into the lines of my face and the years I had lost.

The pain was not wasted. It was translated. Every loss became empathy. Every failure became a warning light I could point out to others before they crashed. Every scar became a tool—a way to guide, to mentor, to lead.

I no longer saw my past as something to escape from. I saw it as inventory—a toolbox filled with hard-earned lessons, forged in fire. The more I shared, the lighter the weight became. What had once felt like chains around my neck became a platform I could stand on.

That reframing was the beginning of purpose. The scars had not made me less—they had equipped me. And in learning to use them, I discovered something powerful: the same things that almost destroyed me were now the things that allowed me to build.

There was a time when my words only lived in chaos. In crowded rooms filled with noise and bravado, I spoke loudly but said nothing that lasted. My voice stirred distraction rather than direction. It carried no weight beyond the next night's escape.

Years later, I found myself standing on that foreign stage—lights bright, microphone heavy, cameras capturing every word and sending them out to countless people. The silence before I spoke pressed against my chest like a reminder: once, I could not control my own chaos. Now, I was speaking into rooms where ideas shaped futures.

But the truth is, the power of my voice was not limited to conferences or television broadcasts. Some of the most transformative moments came before and after trips to Uzbekistan, in face-to-face, one-on-one conversations. Sitting with clients, mentoring younger entrepreneurs, or simply sharing over coffee, I saw the same shift happen: stories cut through. When I spoke about shame, psychosis, or the hollow silence after chaos, people leaned in. Not because I had titles or degrees, but because I spoke a language they understood–the language of pain turned into purpose.

This balance taught me something vital: impact isn't measured by the size of the audience. Whether it was tens of millions on TV or one young person across the table, my story had the same message: transformation is possible.

For years, my mantra had been "I must survive my story." Every decision was about making it through another day. Now the mantra had changed: "I can use my story to help others survive theirs."

That shift turned my voice into vision. It's no longer about me. It's about standing as proof that no matter how far you fall, you can rise, rebuild, and lead.

For a long time, I thought legacy was something other men left behind–fathers to children, leaders to nations, visionaries to history. Me? I was too busy surviving the wreckage I'd made. Legacy felt like a word from a different world.

But as I built businesses, something shifted. These companies were never meant to be mere profit-centers. Money matters, yes, but it's never the end of the story. Each business became an ecosystem–a place where growth could ripple outward. Every employee hired, partner trusted, and contract honored was proof that creation could replace destruction.

I had once believed that my scars disqualified me from leading. Who would trust a man with a past like mine? But I came to understand the opposite: scars are not disqualifiers; they are credentials. They prove survival, resilience, and the ability to rebuild after collapse. When I shared openly with my teams, it did not weaken their trust. It deepened it because they saw not just a CEO, but a human being who had lived through fire and chosen to build anyway.

Purpose, I realized, was no longer about my own survival. It was about creating spaces where others could thrive. My companies became more than businesses; they became platforms for people to see that reinvention is real, that discipline pays off, and that past failures don't dictate future ceilings.

This, to me, is legacy: not statues or titles, but seeds planted in people. Showing through action that transformation is possible, that contribution matters, and that scars can be blueprints for others to rise.

I no longer chase survival. I build ecosystems where others can see themselves not as broken, but as becoming. And if I leave anything behind, let it be this truth: purpose is not about escaping pain; it is about using it to create a future bigger than yourself.

Creativity Redefined

For years, I called myself creative. And I was—but my creativity was destruction in disguise. I could create chaos out of calm, turn trust into suspicion, and spin stories to manipulate my way through almost any door. My creativity lived in fast living, reckless choices, and illusions that burned out as quickly as they were made. It was restless, impulsive, and ultimately hollow.

But transformation taught me something I had never considered before: creativity is not just the ability to invent—it is the discipline to build. For the first time, I began to channel that restless energy into systems, visions, and strategies. Where once I designed excuses, now I design companies and the future. Where once I manipulated for survival, now I negotiate for growth. Where once I built chaos, now I build order.

This was the deepest creative shift of my life. Creativity stopped being about running wild and started being about laying foundations. Every business plan was an act of imagination. Every contract signed was a brushstroke on a canvas larger than me. Even the structures of my companies—the teams, the systems, the partnerships—became works of design. The same mind that once spent its energy outrunning consequences now invests in shaping futures.

And here's the truth I discovered: creativity without discipline collapses. But when creativity is rooted in structure, it becomes unstoppable. That was my transformation—not losing my wildness but taming it, not erasing my imagination but giving it rails to run on.

Today, I see creativity differently. It is not in the noise of a fast night or the rush of reckless living. It is in the quiet work of strategy, the patience of building, the courage to dream beyond survival. Creativity, redefined, is not about escaping reality but constructing one that lasts.

That is the true internal transformation: the same energy that once destroyed me now fuels the systems, visions, and structures that will outlive me.

Pain had once ruled me. It dictated my choices, pushed me into substances, and chained me to survival mode. For years, I believed pain was the enemy, something to outrun, numb, or bury. But standing here now, I see it differently: pain became my fuel. It was the raw material that forced me to grow, the spark that ignited contribution, the voice that made my story worth telling.

Through purpose and contribution, I was transformed. I moved from being a man who barely believed he could stand on his own two feet into someone capable of creating businesses, systems, opportunities, and impact. The same experiences that once disqualified me became the very proof that resilience is real. My scars, once sources of shame, became the credentials that connected me to others who needed hope.

But purpose is not only about surviving your own story; it is about building something that can stand when you are gone. Contribution gave me momentum. Purpose gave me direction. Together, they demanded the next step: creating structures that would last.

That's where the journey turns now. The next chapter is about The Architecture of a New Life—how I turned lessons into systems, visions into strategies, and discipline into freedom. It is about the routines, frameworks, and choices that made the transformation sustainable.

Because pain may light the fire, but only structure keeps it burning. That is where I truly began becoming who I needed to be.

If I Could Talk to My Younger Self

The Power of Your Voice

You'll learn that your voice has power. Not because people clap or because lights shine on you, but because your story will prove transformation is possible. You will stop trying to survive your story and begin using it to help others survive theirs. Speaking, mentoring, even one-on-one conversations—they will matter more than you can imagine right now.

Business as a Platform for Growth

You'll also see that business isn't only about money. You'll build companies that give other opportunities. You will create systems that enable people to grow. Your employees, your partners, even strangers will look at you and see proof that scars don't disqualify a man—they prepare him.

Creativity Transformed

And maybe the biggest shift: your creativity will change. The same energy you once used for destruction—chaos, manipulation, running wild—will become the energy you use to build. You'll design visions, strategies, and systems that last. That's real creativity: not burning everything down but building something that endures.

Pain as Fuel

So don't curse the pain. One day, it will be your fuel.

CHAPTER 10

Becoming Who I Needed To Be

Informal Mentorship

The first time someone leaned across the table and asked, "How did you do it?" I almost laughed. We were sitting in a quiet restaurant, two entrepreneurs sharing lunch, the air filled with the clatter of dishes and the muted hum of conversation. For a second, I didn't know how to answer. Part of me still carried the weight of my past, the chaos, the scars. To have someone see me as a man worth asking for guidance felt surreal.

I set down my fork, looked him in the eye, and said the only truth I knew: "I made a decision to change my life. Then I committed to that decision." It wasn't easy, but it was real. I told him about determination, consistency, and the Finnish concept of *sisu*—that stubborn, almost unshakable inner strength that refuses to quit, even when the odds are against you.

Another time in Vienna, I was having lunch with a friend named Adam Casals when I shared my story—not the polished version, but the raw truth of prison, recovery, and rebuilding. He listened silently, then leaned back and said, "This is a success story." The words landed more heavily than I expected. For so long, I had thought of my life as a wreckage barely pieced together. To someone else, it was proof that change was possible.

Those moments taught me something: mentorship doesn't always begin in classrooms or boardrooms. Sometimes it starts at a lunch table, in an honest conversation, when someone looks at you and sees not just your scars but your survival—and asks how they might find their own way forward.

When people first began asking me for guidance, I wondered why they trusted me. I wasn't the polished academic, nor the seasoned executive with a spotless résumé. I was a man who had stumbled, fallen hard, and spent years climbing out. Yet it was exactly those scars that gave me credibility.

My advice carried weight not because I had read about resilience, but because I had lived through the nights when resilience was the only option. When I spoke about discipline, it wasn't theory; it was the reality of sitting in a prison cell, forcing myself to complete assignments when every instinct told me to give up. When I spoke about sobriety, it wasn't statistics; it was the decision I made in February 2019, drawing a line I refused to cross ever again.

People could feel that difference. The words were not abstract; they were earned. And ironically, the very things I once wanted to hide—psychosis, shame, prison, failed relationships—became the reason others leaned in. My scars became maps for those who felt stuck in their own darkness. They didn't need perfection; they needed proof that broken things could be rebuilt.

I thought back often to my younger self. Back then, when someone older tried to guide me, I dismissed them. I thought they couldn't understand me, that their advice was weakness dressed as wisdom. My arrogance kept me deaf to voices that might have saved me pain. I equated mentorship with control, not realizing that guidance is an act of generosity, not domination.

Now the roles had reversed. I was the one being asked, "How did you do it?" And instead of dismissing the question, I answered with honesty. I didn't hide behind bravado or pretend the journey was smooth. I told the truth: change is possible, but only when decision becomes commitment, and commitment becomes action.

The greatest shift was this: I no longer saw my scars as liabilities. They were assets. They gave me a language that connected not just minds but hearts. They turned me into a mentor without me even chasing the title.

I had once been a man running from every lesson life offered me. Now, I was living proof that even the hardest lessons could be passed on—not as warnings, but as fuel for others to believe in their own transformation.

I knew long before I started companies that leading others would first require learning how to lead myself. When I made the decision to change my life, I also committed to becoming my own leader. Until that moment, I had been reactive, walking through life without a clear purpose or direction, and chasing short-term relief instead of building toward anything lasting.

Self-leadership became the foundation. It was not about dramatic breakthroughs but about small, stubborn acts of consistency: waking up on time and completing assignments when no one was watching, and refusing to quit even when the temptation to escape was strong. For years, I had broken promises to myself, and each broken promise weakened my confidence. Reversing that pattern meant counting small wins until discipline became stronger than impulse.

By the time I began building businesses, this internal leadership had already taken root. My companies are still small, but even a handful of employees or partners look for stability in the person guiding them. And stability cannot be faked. They do not measure me by the size of my office or the title on my business card; instead, they measure me by whether I show up, whether I do what I said I would do, and whether I stay steady under pressure.

That is why I see business as more than profit-making. It is a training ground for character. Every decision I make is a lesson first for myself and then for those who work alongside me. If I drift, they drift. If I stay disciplined, they have an anchor to steady themselves against.

Mentorship in business, as I have lived it, is less about giving instructions and more about modelling a way of being. You cannot preach resilience if you fold when things get hard. You cannot demand consistency if you cut corners in your own work. You cannot ask others to commit if you keep one foot in and one foot out.

I learned to lead myself before I ever dared to lead anyone else. And that lesson became clear: self-leadership is not just preparation for guiding others—it is the mentorship itself. By living with purpose and consistency, you show others it is possible.

I knew long ago that mentorship does not always come with a title. Sometimes it happens in the quietest moments—when someone sits across from you, finally letting down their guard, and speaks about the weight they are carrying. Over the years, I have had countless conversations like that. People have told me more than once, "It's easy to talk to you. I feel lighter, like a heavy burden has dropped off my shoulders."

One conversation stays with me. A friend shared a dream, and something in it caught my attention. I asked carefully, "Do you have self-destructive thoughts?" She looked at me, and tears filled her eyes as she whispered, "Yes." In that moment, my role was not to lecture or fix, but to sit with her honesty, to acknowledge her pain, and to show her that admitting it did not make her weak—it made her ready for change.

I've often guided people in these moments toward simple truths: transformation doesn't begin with giant leaps but with small daily actions. Writing something down, walking instead of drinking, and making one phone call instead of isolating—these are the steps that plant new seeds. I told them that consistency, not perfection, creates change.

And here is another opportunity to share the Finnish concept of *sisu*: the inner strength that awakens when everything else is exhausted, and the quiet determination to keep moving when every part of you wants to quit. It's not about being fearless; it's about holding the line through fear, shame, and fatigue until the tide begins to turn.

This concept isn't meant to be a motivational slogan. I was showing them a truth I had lived: survival alone isn't enough—you need persistence beyond comfort. And persistence, repeated day after day, builds change.

These personal conversations taught me that scars can be transformed into bridges. By sharing my own struggles honestly and offering the tools I had discovered, I wasn't just giving advice. I was giving others what I once needed most: proof that no one is beyond redemption, and that even in the darkest seasons, there is a path forward—one small step, one act of *sisu* at a time.

Mentorship was never something I chased or even imagined myself stepping into. It emerged naturally, in conversations, in quiet moments, and in the unexpected honesty of people who trusted me with their struggles. And what surprised me most was this: while I was offering guidance to others, mentorship was shaping me just as much—maybe more.

Lessons from Old Scars

The first lesson it gave me was accountability. I quickly realized that I couldn't speak about discipline, consistency, or *sisu* if I wasn't living them myself. Every time I encouraged someone to take small daily steps toward change, I heard my own words echo back to me like a mirror. "Stay steady. Stay consistent. Keep going." I could not afford to become a man of empty talk. Mentorship demanded that my actions stay aligned with my advice, and that alignment strengthened me. It became a daily discipline—not just for me, but for those who might look to me as proof.

It also taught me humility. In my younger years, I dismissed mentors, believing I knew better or that their lessons did not apply to me. Now, sitting across from people who shared their fears and destructive thoughts, I understood the weight of being trusted. Their vulnerability reminded me of my own. I was not above them; I was simply a few steps ahead on the same road.

That humility kept me grounded. It reminded me that mentorship is not about status; it's about service.

But perhaps the deepest gift mentorship gave me was validation. For years, I carried my scars as private shame—the psychosis, the losses, the chaos I had created. These were chapters I once wished I could erase. Yet in mentoring moments, those very scars became the bridge that made others open up. When someone cried after admitting self-destructive thoughts, and I could meet them without judgment because I had lived my own version of that darkness, that was when my past began to feel redeemed. Pain was no longer wasted; it had become raw material for connection.

There was nothing more powerful than seeing change unfold in front of me. Sometimes it was subtle: a friend choosing healthier routines after our talks, or an acquaintance telling me that one conversation gave them the strength to try again. Other times, it was more direct: people later came back to tell me, "That talk with you shifted something in me." Every time I heard words like that, the weight of my past felt lighter. What once threatened to destroy me had become a source of life for someone else.

Informal mentorship gave me back my sense of purpose. It reminded me that my journey wasn't just about my own survival or success. It showed me that the discipline I practiced daily was not only protecting my future, but could ripple outward, touching lives I might never have expected.

In the end, mentorship did not just help others. It rewired me. It deepened my resilience, sharpened my discipline, and transformed my scars into tools. It was living proof that the story I once thought disqualified me was, in fact, the very thing that qualified me to serve.

If I Could Talk to My Younger Self

The Power of a Decision

One day, someone will lean across a table and ask, "How did you do it?" And you will not answer with theories or slogans. You will answer with truth: "I made a decision. And I committed to that decision." That is it. No magic. No shortcut. Just determination, consistency, and the quiet force we Finns call sisu.

The Quiet Strength of *Sisu*

Sisu will carry you when strength runs out. It is not loud. It is the stubborn refusal to quit when quitting feels easier. It is finishing assignments in a prison cell when your mind tells you it does not matter. It is choosing sobriety one day, then another, and then another until it becomes your new foundation.

Leadership Begins Within

You will discover that leadership does not begin in boardrooms. It begins when you finally keep a promise to yourself. Every small win—waking up on time, finishing what you started, refusing to escape—will stack into confidence. That is how you will learn to lead yourself, and only then will you be ready to guide others.

Scars Become Bridges

And here is the truth that will surprise you most: the very things you want to hide right now—the scars, the failures, the broken nights—will become bridges. They will open doors into other people's pain, and you'll find yourself mentoring, guiding, or even just sitting with them in silence when they finally let their burden drop.

Mentorship as Presence

You will realize that mentorship is not about having all the answers. It is about being present, honest, and consistent. It is about showing that scars are not stains, but maps.

Your Story as a Gift

So do not run from your story. One day, it will be the reason someone else finds the courage to begin theirs.

Recognizing the Call to Help Others

Ten minutes before I was scheduled to speak in Uzbekistan, I realized my prepared speech would not do. The room I was about to enter demanded more—sharper words, clearer focus, something that rose to the weight of the moment. So, I sat down, pen in hand, and rewrote the entire speech on the spot. No time for hesitation, just pure concentration.

When I walked into the hall, I was on time. My seat was beside the Minister of Labor, with leaders and policymakers from across the world surrounding us. Flags lined the stage, translators adjusted their headsets, and cameras pointed toward the podium. The atmosphere was thick with expectation—the kind that can make even seasoned speakers falter.

Then my name was called. The silence before speaking stretched wide, as if the entire room was holding its breath. For a moment, a flash of my past crossed my mind—the prison cell, the high school assignments, the nights I once drowned in chaos. And then I felt it: this was no longer about survival; this was contribution.

As I began to speak, the words carried more than facts. They carried the scars I had turned into lessons, the discipline I had forged through years of struggle, the proof that transformation was possible. Looking out at the audience, I knew this moment was larger than me. Once, I could barely control my own life. Now, I was shaping conversations that reached across nations.

For years, my life was ruled by survival. Every thought circled around one question: How do I get through this moment? Survival mode makes you self-focused because it feels like there is no room for anything else. But survival, while necessary for a time, is also a cage. You may still be alive, but you are not truly living.

The shift came when I realized life could not stop at saving myself. My scars, my failures, my long nights of struggle—they were not just obstacles. They were tools. Tools that could help me serve others. Serving others became the opposite of survival. Instead of asking, "What do I need right now?" The question became: "What strength can I give right now?"

Sometimes that meant small but decisive actions. I remember once when someone thought he was having heart problems. He was ready to drive himself to the hospital, but I stepped in. I told him, "You are not driving like this. I will take you." I made sure he got to the hospital and received treatment. It was a simple act—no spotlight, no stage—just being there when someone needed it most. But that is what service is: showing up, steady, when someone else cannot carry themselves.

That moment reminded me that service does not drain you—it fills you. Every time I extend a hand, I feel my own strength grow deeper. Every time I carry someone else through their storm, my own past storms make sense.

The old life was about "me first" survival. The new life is about serving. And here is the truth: serving does not just change the one you help. It transforms you. It turns scars into credibility, pain into purpose, and every moment of survival into a foundation for impact.

There was a time when people looked at me and saw only destruction. My reputation was built on chaos—fast nights, reckless choices, scars I did not bother to hide. Back then, if anyone took me as an example, it was as a warning of what not to do. That was my reality, and for years I carried it like a shadow I could not shake.

But something shifted as I rebuilt. Slowly, people stopped asking about the chaos and started asking about the climb. "How did you do it?" "What changed?" Their questions weren't about curiosity—they were about hope. They looked at me—a man who had walked through shame, prison, addiction, and loss—and they saw not just a survivor, but someone who had rebuilt.

That realization came with responsibility. I could no longer speak carelessly, no longer function as if my choices affected only me. Every word, every story I shared carried weight, because people were listening. For some, my journey became a mirror for what they longed for in their own lives. That is not a role to take lightly.

Responsibility meant honesty. I could not sugarcoat the pain or pretend transformation was easy. I had to speak plainly: change is possible, but it takes commitment, discipline, and consistency. Responsibility also meant humility. I was not a hero—I was a man who chose differently and kept choosing. The moment I pretended otherwise, I would lose the very credibility my scars had earned me.

Today, I understand that being seen as an example is not about perfection. It is about showing, again and again, that brokenness can be rebuilt, that scars can become blueprints. My story carries weight, not because it is flawless, but because it proves that change is real.

That responsibility is not a burden. It is a gift—a daily reminder that my life is no longer about destruction. It is about showing what can rise from it.

When I first began to change my life, my "platform" was a small desk in a prison, a pen, and a stack of assignments. I never imagined that one day my words would reach beyond those walls—that they would echo in conference halls, in offices, and even on television screens to millions of people.

The first step in the shift was realizing that something needed to change. The first visible proof of that shift was completing school courses one by one. Speaking at conferences soon became another visible sign of this transformation. I still remember my speaking opportunity in Uzbekistan, sitting beside the Minister of

Labor and surrounded by leaders from across the world. Only a few years earlier, I was a man fighting to control his own chaos. Now, I was giving a speech, and my words carried weight. Cameras broadcasted my message to tens of millions. That moment was surreal—it felt both humbling and expansive at once. I realized that the story I once wanted to bury had become a tool to inspire and to build.

Me having a speech in Uzbekistan.

Media appearances added another layer. Each time I sat in front of a camera, I thought of the boy who once hid his shame in silence. Now, I was not hiding—I was speaking openly, turning scars into proof that transformation is possible. Whether the audience was a boardroom, a group of employees, or viewers across an entire region, the principle was the same: share the truth and show the possibility.

Inside my companies, the platform looked different but mattered just as much. Leading small teams, mentoring employees, and guiding colleagues required the same honesty I continued to demonstrate. People do not only need strategies; they need to see that consistency and discipline are lived, not just taught.

Each platform multiplied my reach, from one-on-one conversations where a heavy burden dropped from someone's shoulders to international broadcasts. The contrast still humbles me: once, my voice was lost in chaos; now, it helps shape order, vision, and courage in others.

The platforms themselves are not the legacy. What matters is the impact they carry—proof that even the most broken beginnings can lead to influence that stretches far beyond what you once imagined.

There came a point when helping others stopped being something I chose to do and started becoming something I had to do. It was no longer a side activity, but a purpose—a call I could not ignore. For years, my life had been about survival: how to get through the next day, the next hour, the next craving. But when I began mentoring, guiding, and simply being present for people, I discovered a new kind of fuel. Helping others anchored me as much as it supported them.

Neuroscience explains why: When we shift our focus from ourselves to others, the brain engages regions tied to empathy and reward—particularly the prefrontal cortex and the mesolimbic system. Contribution creates a loop of meaning: as we help, dopamine and oxytocin reinforce the behavior, giving us not just a sense of connection, but also a sense of purpose. In survival mode, my brain was wired for immediate relief, bracing against danger. In service mode, my brain rewired itself for impact, patience, and building. Contribution literally reshaped my mind, just as discipline had reshaped my life.

But beyond science, there was a simple truth: every time someone shared their burden with me, I felt accountable to live my own words. I could not advise someone to stay consistent if I wasn't consistent myself. I could not tell someone to face their shame if I were hiding from mine. Helping others became a mirror that reflected the discipline I had to maintain. That accountability was a gift—one that kept me grounded when pride or fatigue tried to creep in.

And in each of those moments—whether driving someone to the hospital when they feared heart trouble, or sitting across the table while a friend confessed their destructive thoughts—I realized that my scars had not been wasted. They were signposts. By naming my failures, I gave others permission to face theirs. By showing my recovery, I gave them proof that their own was possible.

Answering the call meant carrying a responsibility bigger than myself. It meant speaking honestly, not sugarcoating the struggle, but also not withholding the hope. My past had once silenced me. Now, it has given me credibility. The very places where I had fallen became the places where I could stand for others.

That is why helping others is not an option for me—it is my purpose. Service became the bridge between who I was and who I am. It turned my story from a survival manual into a roadmap for change.

And yet, the journey does not stop here. Because the people who need this message most are often the ones still searching, still trapped in the same silence I once carried. The next chapter is for them—a letter to the ones still fighting to believe that change is possible.

If I Could Talk to My Younger Self

From Prison Cells to Global Stages

You will not believe this now, but one day you will sit beside ministers, rewriting a speech minutes before walking on stage in front of leaders from around the world. You will hold a microphone steady, your words translated into multiple languages, and you will realize the silence in the room is not waiting for you to fail—it is waiting to hear what you have learned.

Walking Through Chaos First

But before that day comes, you will walk through chaos. You will sit in a cell with math books and psychology papers. You will face nights when shame feels unbearable and silence feels like punishment. You will convince yourself you are broken, disqualified from anything good. But listen closely: you are not broken. You are still forming.

Scars as Credibility

Every scar you collect—psychosis, prison, addiction, failure—will one day become credibility. The very things you want to hide will be the tools that allow you to serve. People will trust you not because you read about resilience, but because you lived it. You will tell them about that stubborn Finnish drive that keeps you moving when everything else collapses, and they will believe you because they will see it in your life.

From Survival to Service

Remember this: survival is not the end goal. Serving is. Survival asks, "What do I need right now?" Service asks, "What strength can I give right now?" And every time you give—whether it is driving a friend to the hospital, helping someone leave an abusive home, or sitting across the table while they confess their darkest thoughts—you will find your own strength deepen.

Proof and Responsibility

One day, people will stop seeing you as a warning and start seeing you as proof. Proof that discipline works. Proof that consistency matters. Proof that scars can become blueprints. And with that proof comes responsibility: to live what you speak, to stay honest, to show that change is possible.

Do Not Give Up

So please do not give up on the nights when it feels hopeless. Do not drown the silence. Do not run from your scars. Every choice to endure, to act, to keep your word—those are the building blocks of the man you will become.

Your Story as a Bridge

And when you get there, remember: your story is not for you alone. It is the bridge someone else needs to cross.

PART THREE

THE MESSAGE

CHAPTER 11

A Letter to the Ones Still Searching

If You Are Feeling Lost, This Is For You

If you are reading this, there's a good chance you've been fighting battles no one else sees. The kind that keeps you awake at night, staring at the ceiling while your chest tightens and your thoughts won't stop. You know how to smile in the daylight, how to play the part, how to tell people you're "fine"–but inside, it feels like you're crumbling. Maybe you numb it with alcohol, drugs, food, endless noise, or distraction. Maybe you keep running, hoping that if you move fast enough, the heaviness won't catch you.

I know that weight. I know what it's like to feel ashamed of the things you've done, the opportunities wasted, and the chaos you created. I know the restless nights when silence feels louder than any crowd. I know the loneliness of carrying all of it inside, afraid that if anyone saw the truth, they'd turn away.

So let me tell you something that took me years to learn: if you are lost, this is for you. You are not reading these words by accident. Whatever road brought you here–pain, confusion, failure, searching–has led you to this moment for a reason. You are not broken beyond repair. You are not too far gone. Being lost does not mean the story is over. It means the story is still unfolding.

This chapter is my letter to you–a hand extended in the dark, a reminder that the path forward begins not with perfection but with possibility.

I want to name the feelings you might not even have words for yet, because I know how heavy it is to carry them alone.

Shame is the first one. It clings like a shadow, whispering that you are less than others, that you are disqualified from belonging. Shame does not just remind you of mistakes; it convinces you that you are the mistake. It's the voice that makes your eyes drop to the ground when you should be looking forward. I know that voice—it haunted me for years.

Then there's anxiety. It does not always look like a panic attack. Sometimes it's quieter but relentless: a tight chest, shallow breaths, the restless racing of thoughts you cannot slow down. Anxiety tells you that something is wrong, even when you are sitting still. It makes rest feel impossible. I know that feeling; I used to think my own heartbeat might give me away to the guards outside my cell.

And grief. Not just grief for people you have lost, but grief for time wasted, for relationships broken, for the person you wish you had been. Grief is like carrying a backpack filled with rocks everywhere you go. No matter how you try to set it down, it is always there, pressing you into the ground. I know that weight; I carried it for years before I learned how to let it pass through me.

If you feel any of these, let me tell you this: you are not weak for feeling them. You are human. These emotions are not proof of your failure; they are signals, reminders that you are alive and still capable of change.

I can name them because I have lived them. I sat where you sit, with shame, anxiety, and grief pressing me from every side. And if there is one thing I want you to hear, it's this: those feelings are not your executioners. They are not the end of you. They are the beginning of transformation.

If you are holding this right now, I need you to know something: feeling lost does not mean the end. It does not mean you are broken beyond repair. It means you are standing at the beginning of a different road, even if you cannot see where it leads.

I know how heavy it feels. Shame sits in your chest like a stone. Anxiety rattles your breath until you cannot catch it. Grief presses against your ribs like a weight you cannot set down. When you are in that place, the idea of starting again feels impossible.

But here is the truth: you do not need to see the whole road; you only need to take the next step.

The Quiet Determination to Carry On

I had to lean on *sisu* when I started high school in prison at thirty-eight years old. Shame screamed that I was too late, that I was a failure compared to everyone else my age. Sitting in that cell with schoolbooks, I felt ridiculous. But I made myself finish one page. Then another. I told myself: do not look at the whole mountain. Just climb the next step. And slowly, step by step, something shifted. Each assignment I completed was proof that shame was not stronger than persistence.

That same *sisu* lives in you, even if you cannot see it yet. Even if your story feels shattered, it is already there—waiting for you to take that first honest step.

So be honest with yourself—name where you are. Admit what hurts. Stop running from the silence. That honesty will awaken something inside: the quiet fire that says, I am not done yet.

You do not need to fix everything tonight. You do not need to know how it all ends. You need to take the next small step. That is how new lives begin.

If you are waiting for a lightning bolt, a sudden miracle that will wipe away the pain and rewrite your life in an instant—let me save you some time. It does not work like that. Change does not arrive as a single explosion. It arrives as a series of stubborn, quiet choices stacked on top of one another until they begin to build a new foundation.

I know this because that is how I lived it. When I was thirty-eight years old, I sat in a prison cell with books of psychology and mathematics spread out on the desk. It did not feel like I was doing something exhilarating. It was just me, fluorescent light buzzing overhead, pages that seemed too heavy for my tired mind, and years of shame pressing down on my shoulders. But I made the choice to begin. Not to finish everything at once, not to map out ten years ahead—just to open the book and take the first step. That moment did not change my life overnight, but it planted the seed of everything that followed.

Psychology gave me language for what I had carried in silence. Words like shame, anxiety, and grief stopped being vague storms and became signals I could name and observe. Every chapter I studied felt like a small torch lit in a dark room.

Mathematics gave me something else: patience. It taught me that problems do not bend to force or frustration. They yield when you break them down step by step, when you trust the process more than the rush. That lesson was bigger than numbers. It became a way to approach life itself.

The same principle held true with sobriety. I did not reach freedom by imagining the rest of my life alcohol-free in one sweep. I did it by choosing one sober night, then another, and another. Each small decision was like laying one brick. Alone, it did not look like much. But piled together over time, those bricks became walls strong enough to build a new life inside.

Even journaling began that way. My first entries were not polished insights. They were fragments, scribbles, half-sentences. But they were honest. And honesty, repeated over days and weeks, grew into self-understanding.

I want you to know this: you do not need to perform perfection. You do not need to fix everything by tomorrow. All you need is to choose one action today that points forward. Then repeat it. Progress is not measured in leaps but in steps.

Consistency beats intensity. Small choices, made stubbornly, are what carry you through. That is the truth of transformation: no miracles, only momentum.

Failure as a Necessary Step

Let us be honest: failure is part of the journey. You will stumble. You will take two steps forward and one step back. You will wake up some days and feel like all your progress has slipped through your fingers. I know because I lived it.

When I was released from prison, I did not walk out as a finished product. I did not instantly stop drinking or leave every old pattern behind. For a while, I still used alcohol and substances on certain occasions. At first, those moments felt like proof that I was doomed to repeat my past. Shame whispered: See, nothing has changed. But over time, I realized something crucial: relapse was not finality. It was feedback.

Each slip showed me something about myself. It revealed where my boundaries were weak, where my environment pulled me back, and where I still needed to build strength. And each time I recommitted, I grew a little stronger. Not because I erased failure, but because I refused to let it define me.

That is how resilience is built—not in the absence of setbacks, but in the act of standing back up again and again. Every recommitment was like tempering steel: heated, struck, cooled, and made stronger.

So if you stumble, do not waste energy on self-condemnation. Ask instead: What is this teaching me? Failure does not mean you are broken beyond repair. It means you are human. It means you are learning.

The truth is, the people who succeed are not those who never fall. They are the ones who keep getting back up, who treat each failure as a teacher instead of a verdict. That is what I had to learn, and it is what I want you to carry: failure is not the end of your story. It is the part that makes the next chapter possible.

If you are reading this and you feel lost, hear me clearly: lost is not the end of the story. Lost is where the map begins. It is the place where you stop pretending you already know the way and start learning how to walk differently.

I know how heavy it feels—the shame, the setbacks, the silence when you wonder if anyone else could ever understand. I know the nights when you sit with your thoughts, and they feel like enemies. But I also know this: those same nights can be the soil where something new begins to grow.

Every choice you make, no matter how small—opening a book, writing one line in a journal, choosing one sober night—is a seed. At first, it looks like nothing. But over time, those seeds grow roots. And those roots can carry you through storms you never thought you could survive.

You are not too late. You are not beyond repair. You are not defined by your lowest moments. You are simply standing at the starting line of a new chapter.

And that is where we go next. Because the truth is not just that you are lost. The truth is deeper: you are not broken; you are simply early in your story.

You Are Not Broken, Just Early in the Story

I know you think you are broken. I thought the same about myself. I looked at the wreckage of my past—the failures, the shame, the moments I thought I would never rise from—and believed I was beyond repair. But here is the truth I wish someone had told me then: you are not broken. You are still forming.

Think of it like a building under construction. From the outside, it can look chaotic: scaffolding everywhere, dust in the air, unfinished walls, and piles of materials lying around. To someone just passing by, it may look like a mess, maybe even like ruins. But the builder knows what is taking shape. The structure is there. The foundations are being laid. The mess is not destruction—it's creation in progress.

That is what you are—a work in progress. The pain you feel, the confusion, and even the setbacks are not signs of failure. They are signs that something deeper is being built inside you. The chaos you see now is not your end. It is the scaffolding of your future.

I used to believe my scars disqualified me. But I later discovered they were proof that I had survived long enough to grow stronger. You may feel early in your story, still stumbling, still piecing things together—but that does not mean broken. It means you are becoming.

And becoming is far more powerful than pretending to be finished.

Shame has a way of whispering lies so convincingly that we start to believe them. Addiction reinforces the lie with every relapse. Trauma stamps it deeper, convincing us that what happened to us, or what we have done, means we are defective. The story we tell ourselves becomes real.

I know that story well. I remember sitting at a small desk in a prison, staring at a blank page where an essay assignment was supposed to take shape. The fluorescent light above flickered, and my pen hovered uselessly over the paper. My mind told me, "You do not belong here. Others your age are leading teams, raising families, and building lives. And here you are, almost forty years old, struggling to write a paragraph." At that moment, I was certain I was broken, too late to matter.

But here is what I learned: what feels like failure in the moment is often the very foundation you will build on later. That blank page—and the persistence to fill it anyway—became a training ground.

Those faltering steps were not proof of brokenness but of what I was rebuilding.

The perception is that scars and setbacks are disqualifiers. The truth is, they are credentials. They do not make you worthless; they make you real. They do not mean you are broken; they mean you've been tested.

What looks like a collapse can be the excavation before construction. The ground has to be dug up, the dirt cleared, and the cracks exposed before a foundation can be poured. That's what many of us mistake for being broken—we're in the excavation stage, and all we can see is the dirt.

You may feel defective, but you are not. You are being prepared. Your story is not over—it is still under construction. And the illusion of brokenness fades the moment you realize the mess is not the end, but the beginning of a stronger structure.

Scars have a way of making us want to cover them. We hide them under clothes, silence, or distraction, hoping no one will notice where we've been cut, bruised, or broken. For years, I carried scars like that—not only the visible ones, but the invisible ones carved by shame, psychosis, and prison walls. I thought they were marks of failure, proof that I was beyond repair.

But here is what I discovered: scars do not disqualify you. They prepare you.

Take psychosis, for example. In the middle of that storm, when my thoughts were twisted and the world blurred, I had a single, startling moment of clarity: I am in psychosis. That recognition, that ability to observe even while inside the chaos, became a tool I carried forward. Later, when I studied psychology, I used the same skill—self-observation—to reflect on my past and make decisions that shaped my future. That scar became a blueprint.

Shame worked the same way. For most of my life, shame was a voice telling me I was worthless. In prison, I had to sit with it. My cheeks burned, my stomach sank, but instead of running, I stayed. And when I stayed, I realized shame was not an executioner—it was a signal, a reminder of my need for connection. That painful scar became the foundation for empathy. When someone now sits across from me, drowning in their own shame, I can look them in the eye and say, "I know. I have been there. And you can survive this." That is not theory—it has lived truth.

Prison itself was another scar. Bars, routines, the constant awareness of confinement—they stripped me bare. At the time, I thought it was pure punishment. But later, I saw the blueprint: prison gave me the stillness I had always avoided. That enforced silence became the space where I learned to study, to plan, to imagine a different life. The scar of confinement became the map to freedom.

Every painful chapter I once wished I could erase became part of the architecture of my new life. The shame gave me compassion. The psychosis gave me self-awareness. The prison gave me patience and strategy.

You see, scars are not random marks of suffering. They are blueprints. They carry lessons etched in pain, instructions written in struggle. And when you trace them with honesty, they show you how to build stronger, steadier, wiser.

So do not cover your scars. Do not dismiss them as wasted years or permanent damage. They are the evidence that you have survived, and they are the designs you will use to create. My scars once ruled me. Now, they guide me. And yours can do the same. So, if you feel broken, remember that what you really are is unfinished. Your brain is still writing new scripts. Your story is still forming. And every time you choose growth, no matter how small, you are proving that becoming is not just possible—it is inevitable.

When you feel broken, it is easy to believe nothing can change. That voice in your head says, "This is just who I am. This is permanent." But science tells a different story. Neuroscience has a word for it: neuroplasticity. It means your brain is not fixed–it is always adapting, always rewiring, always becoming.

For most of my life, my brain was wired for survival. That meant reacting fast, numbing pain, chasing short-term relief. The amygdala–the brain's alarm system–was running the show. It fired every time anxiety clenched my chest, or shame burned my face. My circuits screamed: escape, numb, fight, repeat. That was survival mode. It kept me alive, but it never let me grow.

Then something changed. In prison, sitting with math problems and psychology books, I forced myself to slow down. Each equation and each paragraph was like a workout for my brain. I did not know it then, but I was building my prefrontal cortex–the part of the brain that plans, regulates, and thinks long-term. Every time I resisted the urge to bolt and instead solved a problem or finished an assignment, I was literally rewiring myself.

It was like stacking bricks. Each formula solved, each journal entry written, each page of psychology studied became a single brick. On their own, they seemed small, almost meaningless. But brick by brick, a new foundation was forming. The old house–the one built on chaos, substances, and running–had collapsed. Now I was laying neural bricks for something solid, something lasting.

This process was repetitive and sometimes painfully slow. Training my brain was no different than physical training; progress comes through repetition. At first, you see nothing. Then, over time, the small choices accumulate. The more you practice patience, honesty, or discipline, the stronger those pathways become. The more you let old impulses pass without obeying them, the weaker those survival circuits get.

Here is the truth: you are not stuck. You are in training. Your brain is learning from every choice you make–one sober night, one page studied, one honest conversation. Over time, those choices shift your brain from survival mode to growth mode.

Survival mode is like a locked room where the only focus is escape. Growth mode is like building a house—slow, steady, one brick at a time. Neuroplasticity means you always have the tools to build, no matter how many times you have torn the house down before.

So if you feel broken, remember that your brain is still writing new scripts. Your story is still forming. And every time you choose growth, no matter how small, you are proving that becoming is not just possible—it is inevitable.

If you are reading this and wondering whether change is worth the fight, let me tell you this: the very energy you once used to destroy yourself is the same energy you can use to build a life beyond anything you imagine. The drive that once went into chaos, running, numbing, or breaking rules, does not vanish. It is still inside you, waiting to be redirected.

I know, because I lived it. For years, I poured all my strength into surviving—through substances, lies, reckless choices. That same restless fire, once I committed to a different direction, became the fuel for finishing high school at forty, earning two master's degrees, building companies, and even standing on international stages. The intensity had not disappeared. It simply found a new purpose.

That is the truth I want you to see: you are not weak. You are not broken. You are powerful—but your power has been misdirected. The moment you choose to commit, everything shifts. The energy you used to escape can become the energy you use to endure, to create, to lead.

Picture this: instead of waking up ashamed, you wake up with purpose. Instead of avoiding responsibility, you carry it proudly—for your education, your work, your relationships. Imagine channelling your discipline into building businesses, into loving deeply, into making an impact that echoes far beyond your own life. That is not a fantasy. That is what your future self is waiting for.

Do not leave your future self behind. He is stronger than you know, wiser than you believe, and he needs you to make the choice today. Every step you take toward discipline, honesty, and persistence is a step closer to meeting him.

Your scars are not chains. They are blueprints. And if you commit, they will guide you into a life where your story is not just about survival—it is about creation, love, and impact.

If I could sit across from you right now, I would tell you this plainly: you are not broken. You are becoming. Every scar, every restless night, every moment you thought you could not go on—it is shaping you into someone the world needs.

I know it feels messy. Construction always does. When a building is half-finished, it does not look beautiful—it looks chaotic, with scaffolding and raw edges exposed. But that does not mean it is falling apart. It means it is not finished yet. And neither are you.

You carry strength inside you that you cannot yet see. I know, because I could not see mine either. It took years of small steps, of refusing to give up, of choosing honesty over escape. But each choice laid a brick, and eventually, the foundation became clear.

Hold on. Stay in the fight. You are not behind. You are not disqualified. You are in the middle of becoming, and the world is waiting for what you carry.

That is why in the next chapter, we will step into the question you might be asking right now: If I do not have a map, how do I find direction? Chapter 12 is about learning to move forward even when no guide is present and discovering that you already carry more guidance than you think.

How to Find Direction Without a Guide

Tactics for Discovering Purpose from Within

The night was quiet—the kind that sharpens every sound. I sat at a small desk, a single lamp spilling light across scattered papers and notebooks filled with half-sentences, lists, and fragments of plans. Outside the window, darkness pressed against the glass, broken only by the faint outline of trees swaying in the night breeze. It was one of those hours when the world feels suspended, when silence demands honesty.

I stared at the page in front of me, waiting for words, waiting for direction. For most of my life, I had looked for someone to tell me what to do—a mentor, a teacher, or maybe a leader who could hand me a map. But in that moment, I realized no one was coming. There was no guide waiting at the door, no hand to draw the lines of my future. The weight and the freedom of that truth landed in my chest at once.

Fear came first—the sharp thought that maybe I was not enough, that maybe I would lose my way without someone to follow. But underneath it stirred something else: freedom. If no one was coming, then nothing stood in the way of me creating my own path. The page in front of me was blank, yes, but that meant it was also open.

That night, alone with pen and silence, I accepted something essential: the guide I had been waiting for was not outside of me. It was within me—and it was time to learn how to listen.

For much of my life, silence had been the enemy. When the noise faded, the memories rushed in—shame, grief, anxiety. That was why I drowned it with alcohol, substances, distractions. But when I began to strip those away, silence stopped being a threat and slowly became a teacher.

I learned this most clearly through journaling. At first, it was nothing more than scribbles—half-thoughts, fragments of sentences, anger spilled on paper. But the more I returned to the notebook, the more I saw patterns. Themes began to repeat: my hunger for stability, my desire to build instead of destroy, and my need for connection. It was as if my life, scattered in fragments, was piecing itself together in ink.

Still, I had to learn an important truth: the mind is not always a faithful messenger. Left unchecked, it produces everything—lies, fears, self-sabotage. If I believed every thought I wrote down, I would have stayed stuck. That is where reflection came in. I did not just write—I read my words back, challenged them, asked myself: Is this truth, or is this fear speaking?

Over time, I began to separate the noise from the signal. The noise was shame repeating old scripts: You are too late. You will never belong. The signal was the values that kept returning, even when I doubted myself: discipline, honesty, and contribution. Naming those values was like finding a compass. They did not tell me the entire map, but they pointed me in the right direction.

Silence became guidance, not because it gave me easy answers, but because it gave me space to hear myself clearly—the real self underneath the chaos. Journaling, reflection, and even quiet walks by the lake all became ways of listening inward.

But listening inward was not passive. It demanded discipline. I had to show up at the page even when I did not feel like it, to sit with discomfort instead of rushing away. I had to learn to be a student and a critic of my own mind at the same time—open enough to hear, sharp enough to question. *What I discovered is this: your inner voice can be a liar, but it can also be a guide. The difference is whether you treat it as absolute or as material to work with. My notebook became that workshop—a place to sift through raw thoughts until the values underneath revealed themselves.*

And once I named those values, I no longer felt lost. I had something to hold onto—a compass I could carry even when no map was in sight.

Purpose is not something you stumble on fully formed, like a hidden treasure chest buried in the sand. It is discovered in pieces, through action. For years, I waited for a clear sign, some thunderclap revelation that would tell me why I was here. It never came. What came instead were opportunities to take small steps—experiments that, over time, pointed me toward meaning.

One of the first experiments was enrolling in high school from prison at thirty-eight. On paper, it was simply education. But in practice, it was testing whether I still had the patience to build something slowly. Every assignment finished and course completed was proof that discipline was possible, and each proof strengthened my sense of direction. It was not just schoolwork; it was me rewriting my story through stubborn repetition.

Then came the decision to build my first company in 2018. The business was small, but it carried symbolic weight. I had spent years destroying things—relationships, trust, even myself. Creating a company was the opposite: an act of building. It was an experiment in responsibility, testing whether I could turn knowledge into value, and whether I could trust myself to carry commitments beyond my own survival. That first company became a clue: maybe my purpose was not only to rebuild my own life, but to build things that could outlast me.

Other experiments came in the form of speaking opportunities. Standing in Uzbekistan, rewriting a speech ten minutes before walking on stage, I felt the weight of influence pressing on me. That moment was not just about performance; it was about service. Could my story, once a chain around my neck, become a key for others? The answer arrived in the faces listening, in the quiet after the words landed. Speaking was not about recognition—it was another test. Another clue.

Each experiment—school, business, speaking—taught me something. Some doors opened, some closed, but all of them revealed patterns. The pattern was clear: purpose is not found by waiting. It is revealed by doing.

The brain is not a fixed machine; it is plastic, meaning it rewires based on what we repeatedly do. When life is lived in survival mode, the brain's circuitry becomes narrow: avoid pain, chase relief, repeat. The amygdala dominates; the prefrontal cortex (responsible for planning and vision) stays quiet.

But every time I chose a new action—opening a textbook, finishing an assignment, drafting a business plan, speaking publicly—I was forcing my brain to fire different circuits. Neuroplasticity works like this: neurons that fire together wire together. Each experiment carved a new groove, making long-term thinking more natural, less foreign.

Even training, which I had done my whole life, reinforced this principle. Physical training is repetition, from showing up, breaking down, to rebuilding. The same applies to the mind. Each act of discipline in study or business was like a mental repetition, strengthening circuits for patience, persistence, and vision.

The analogy is simple: purpose is not discovered in a flash of insight. It is trained into existence, one deliberate act at a time.

For a long time, I thought my scars were proof that I had failed. Psychosis, prison, addiction—they felt like disqualifiers. Who would take advice from a man who had been locked away, who had lost control of his mind, who had burned years in chaos? Shame told me these scars were marks of weakness. But over time, I learned to see them differently. Scars are not the end of a story. They are signposts. They prove you survived, and they carry lessons no textbook can offer.

Psychosis, for example, was once a nightmare I wanted to erase. The confusion, the fear, the sense of losing myself—it was terrifying. Yet from that experience, I learned the skill of self-observation. In the middle of chaos, I had learned to watch my own mind from the outside. Later, when I studied psychology, I realized that skill was powerful. I could use it to reflect on my past, to regulate my present, and to shape my future. The very thing that once felt like a curse became a tool.

Prison was another scar. I used to see it as wasted time, as proof of failure. But sitting in those cells forced me into stillness I had never chosen. It stripped away the noise, the chaos, the escapes. In that stillness, I found space to study, to plan, to face myself. When I speak to people today—whether an employee, a peer, or someone quietly wrestling with their own shame—they do not need theory from me. They trust me because I have lived the silence of the cell, the heaviness of regret, and the discipline it takes to begin again.

Addiction was no different. For years, I thought it was my greatest weakness. But when I finally broke free, people began to ask me how. Not out of curiosity, but because they wanted hope for themselves. My scars became proof. I could say, "I know what it feels like to crave escape. I know what it feels like to believe you cannot stop. But I also know what happens when you choose again, and again, and again to stay the course." That honesty created a connection. And the connection created an impact.

The paradox is this: scars that once convinced me I was broken became the very reasons people trusted me. They were not looking for someone who had lived a perfect life. They were looking for someone who had stumbled, bled, fallen—and still stood back up.

Today, I do not hide my scars. I show them, because scars do not disqualify you; they prepare you. They are proof that the lessons you carry are not theoretical—they are lived, tested, and real.

My scars taught me something vital: meaning is not found in spite of pain. Meaning is found through it.

When something painful happens, the brain does not just store the facts—it encodes the emotion tied to the event. That is why memories of shame, grief, or failure can still trigger the body years later, tightening the chest or flooding the face with heat. The amygdala (the brain's alarm system) tags those memories with "danger," and each time we revisit them, it replays the same stress response.

But here is the breakthrough: neuroscience shows that how we interpret a memory changes the way it lives in the brain. This is called reconsolidation. When you recall a memory and then reframe its meaning—for example, shifting from "this proves I am broken" to "this prepared me to help others"—you are literally altering the emotional weight of that memory. The facts remain, but the sting weakens. Over time, the brain learns to attach new signals: not fear, but resilience; not shame, but strength.

In my own story, prison, psychosis, and shame once replayed as endless evidence of failure. But when I began using those scars as examples to tell my story and applied them to my daily actions, my brain rewired the weight of those memories. They no longer crushed me—they fueled me.

This is why reframing matters. Trauma is not erased, but it can be transformed. The past stops being a chain and becomes a blueprint instead.

Change never begins by accident. It begins with a moment of recognition: the realisation that something must shift. That spark— the awareness that the old way can't continue—is where every transformation starts. But awareness alone is not enough. What comes next is commitment, and after that, action. And when the action feels heavier than you thought you could carry, that's where *sisu*—the Finnish spirit of quiet determination—steps in.

So how do you turn recognition into change? Start small, start practical:

1. Write down three core values.

Ask yourself: What matters most when everything else is stripped away? Is it integrity? Growth? Service? Family? Discipline? Naming these values anchors you. Without them, it's too easy to drift with whatever feels comfortable in the moment. With them, you have a compass.

2. Ask: "If I stripped away fear, what would I want to create?"

Fear keeps most people circling the same ground. Write this question in your journal and answer it honestly. Not what others expect from you. Not what feels safe. But what you would reach for if fear were not calling the shots.

3. Take daily micro-steps.

Transformation is not built in leaps. It is built on stubborn, consistent choices. One assignment finished. One journal entry written. One sober night. One honest conversation. Micro-steps might feel small, but over time, they develop into strength.

And here is the critical piece: when setbacks come—and they will—recommit. Do not waste energy on perfection. Focus on consistency. Every time you return to your values, your vision, and your next step, you train your mind and body to align with the life you are building.

Recognition. Commitment. Action. *Sisu*. That is the rhythm. That is how you discover purpose from within.

The Guide Within You

If I could hand you one truth, it would be this: the guide you keep waiting for may already be within you. Not a perfect mentor who answers every question, not a map that shows every step, but a compass—your values, your scars, your hunger to build something better. That compass has been there all along; you just needed the silence, the honesty, and the courage to listen.

I learned this sitting alone with notebooks in prison, writing through the noise in my own head until patterns began to emerge. I learned it again when I took small risks—enrolling in high school, sketching out my first company, speaking when I felt unqualified. Each time, it was not someone else pointing the way; it was me deciding to move forward, even with uncertainty.

The guide is already inside you. It does not shout; it whispers. It does not show you the whole road; it gives you the strength for the next step. And when you take that step, the next one reveals itself.

But here is the truth: finding purpose is only the beginning. To sustain it, you need something deeper—the daily muscle of discipline, the long horizon of patience, and the courage to trust your gut when the path feels uncertain.

That is where we go next.

Discipline, Patience, and Gut Feelings

Walking out of prison felt like stepping from night into day. When I had gone in, my life was shrouded in darkness—chaos, addiction, and a mind running in endless loops of survival. The walls had been cold, the routines harsh, but within them I had found something unexpected: stillness. In that enforced stillness, I began to rebuild.

The day I was released, the world felt almost blinding. The air outside seemed sharper, the light almost too bright, as if my eyes were not used to hope. But the real test was not freedom itself—it was whether I could carry the discipline I had built inside into this new life, where no one was watching me anymore.

I remember sitting at a desk, no bars on the windows now, no guards pacing the halls. Just me, a lamp glowing over scattered textbooks and notebooks, pages filled with psychology theories, math equations, and outlines of business plans. The silence was different here. Inside prison, silence had been heavy, almost suffocating. Outside, it was full of possibilities—but also responsibility. No one was forcing me to study. No one was checking if I stayed sober. The choice was mine alone.

It struck me that I had entered prison on the darkest night of my life, but I was leaving with the first light of dawn breaking inside me. And I knew: if I wanted that daylight to last, I had to keep showing up, hour by hour, choice by choice. Freedom was not a finish line. It was the beginning of a new day.

When people hear about transformation, they often imagine one grand moment—a flash of clarity, a powerful decision, a breakthrough that instantly rewrites the story. But real change does not work like that. Real change is built brick by brick, through the kind of daily choices that seem almost invisible in the moment.

For me, discipline became the anchor. It was not glamorous. It did not come with applause. It looked like sitting down to complete a high school assignment late at night, even when my body was tired and my mind restless. It looked like opening a math textbook after a long day of work, pushing myself to wrestle with problems I had not touched in decades. It looked like showing up for myself, again and again, when no one else was watching.

At first, the temptation to drift was strong. Inside the prison, a structure was imposed. There were walls, rules, and routines that kept me contained. But once I stepped outside, the walls were gone. No one cared if I stayed sober. No one cared if I finished an assignment or let it slide. Freedom was exhilarating—but it was also dangerous. Without discipline, freedom can quickly collapse back into chaos. That is where small habits saved me: one course, one assignment, and one sober night at a time. Each choice was a compass, pointing me toward the man I wanted to become. Without it, I would have drifted back into old waters. With it, I discovered that consistency has a power stronger than willpower alone—it creates momentum.

Discipline, I learned, is not punishment. It is not about chaining yourself to routines for the sake of rules. Discipline is a form of freedom. It is the structure that protects you from the pull of old habits, the framework that allows growth to take root. Every time I chose to stay the course—to complete the assignment, to finish the task, to keep the promise to myself—I was laying another stone in the foundation of my new life.

Change was subtle at first. No one could see the difference when I stayed up late to write an essay instead of numbing myself with distractions. No one noticed when I refused shortcuts and put in the hours of reading, writing, and reflecting. But over time, those small acts stacked up. They became proof. And proof is stronger than motivation. Motivation comes and goes, but proof stays, reminding you: you can trust yourself.

Discipline is like a compass in a storm. Without it, you are tossed by waves of emotion, fatigue, and temptation. With it, you may not always move fast, but you keep moving in the right direction. For me, that compass pointed toward education, sobriety, and entrepreneurship. It pointed me toward a life where I was no longer reacting to the chaos but building something that could last.

Looking back, I see that discipline was the invisible thread weaving everything together. It did not make my journey easy. But it made it possible.

Discipline is not just a mindset—it is a biological process. Every repeated action strengthens connections in the brain, like carving a deeper groove into a path. Neuroscientists call this neuroplasticity, the brain's ability to adapt and rewire based on experience.

For years, my survival patterns had wired me for immediacy. Substances, chaos, and quick fixes all trained my brain's reward system to seek instant relief. That loop was reinforced by dopamine, a powerful chemical that spikes when we get fast rewards but fades just as quickly.

Discipline created a new loop. Each time I sat with a math problem instead of escaping it and completed an assignment instead of numbing myself, my prefrontal cortex—the part of the brain responsible for planning, patience, and self-control—grew stronger. Over time, the brain begins to prefer the slower, steadier dopamine rewards that come from progress and completion.

Even small, repeated acts—finishing a page of notes, showing up sober for another night, sticking to a routine—signal to the brain: this is the path we are choosing now. And with enough repetition, the old survival circuits weaken while the new growth circuits take over.

The science confirmed what I was living: discipline is not just about willpower. It's about rewiring the brain so that persistence feels natural, and drifting back into chaos feels less and less like home.

The hardest part of change was not the effort—it was the waiting. I wanted the transformation to happen overnight. After my release in 2017, I imagined a clean break, a life instantly remade. But life does not bend to sudden declarations. Real growth requires time, and time is often the heaviest weight to carry.

Between 2017 and 2019, I lived in the tension of "almost." I had cut ties with old circles, reduced my use of alcohol and substances, and built routines that kept me moving forward. But I had not yet committed fully. It took until February 2019—when the bucket of old habits finally overflowed—for me to turn absolutist, to draw a firm line in the sand. Those two years felt slow, frustrating, and even humiliating at times. I wanted to be free of it all instantly. But in hindsight, those years were preparation. They taught me how to walk steadily, not sprint blindly.

Patience proved itself again in education. When I started high school courses in prison, I was already thirty-eight. The last milestone, graduating with a Master of Laws in 2025, was eight years after I first cracked open a Swedish test in prison. Eight years. Nearly a decade of work, study, setbacks, recommitments, and persistence.

But patience was not only about books; it also became the engine of my entrepreneurship. My first company started modestly, and results did not arrive instantly. There were late nights with no income, doubts about whether clients would ever come, and endless hours of groundwork that no one else saw. But just as with education, patience was the compass. Each year is built on the last, teaching me new lessons, expanding my reach, and proving that real growth is cumulative.

This process taught me something vital: impatience destroys businesses the same way it destroys sobriety. If you expect results too fast, you cut corners, make reckless decisions, or give up altogether. But patience—staying the course when the returns are not yet visible—allows a company to root itself deeply enough to grow. Just as in the gym, where muscles grow only after months of unseen repetitions, businesses flourish when consistency outlasts frustration.

Then there's my favorite word: *sisu*. It is what kept me in the chair when I was tired of studying. It was what steadied me when the early businesses felt too small compared to my ambitions. With sisu, patience became endurance in motion. I was not just waiting for life to change—I was building it step by step, even when progress was invisible.

I used to think patience was passive. Now I know it is one of the most active forces in growth. Patience is like training a muscle. Every time you resist the urge to quit, every time you keep working when results are still far away, you are adding another rep. Slowly, the muscle of resilience grows. And just like in training, the growth doesn't show up immediately, but if you stay consistent, one day you'll look back and realize the weight that once crushed you is now something you can carry with ease.

The frustration of wanting change overnight never fully disappears. Even today, I sometimes wish for faster results. But patience taught me that delay does not mean denial. The gap between 2017 and 2025 was not empty space—it was the proving ground that made lasting transformation, in both education and business, possible.

The brain is wired to crave immediate rewards. Every quick fix—a drink, a drug, even scrolling a phone—triggers dopamine, the chemical of anticipation and pleasure. That is why survival mode feels addictive: it rewards now, not later. But patience, practiced over time, rewires this system.

When you delay gratification—finishing a course instead of escaping into distraction, saving money instead of spending it, or choosing sobriety one day at a time—the prefrontal cortex (the part of the brain responsible for planning and self-control) strengthens. Research shows that with repetition, the brain shifts its dopamine response from instant relief to long-term progress.

In simple terms, the more you practice patience, the more your brain learns to enjoy the process instead of just the outcome. That is why *sisu* matters. It keeps you steady long enough for your brain to update its wiring—so that perseverance itself starts to feel rewarding.

Not every decision in my journey came from logic, books, or strategy. Some of the most important ones came from a place deeper than thought—from the gut.

Listening to Your Inner Compass

Intuition is often misunderstood as a mystical force. In reality, it is the brain's way of processing thousands of subconscious patterns built from experience. It is the quiet voice that speaks before the mind has time to argue. For me, it became a compass when the map was not clear.

Cutting ties with my old circles after leaving prison did not make sense at the time. These were people I had known for years. But my gut told me the truth before my mind wanted to accept it: if I stayed, I would be pulled back into chaos. It was brutal, like cutting away a piece of myself. But I listened, and that decision saved me.

The same silent guide helped me in business. Not every deal looked good on the surface, but the gut knows when something does not add up—the tone in someone's voice, the hesitation behind their promises, or the feeling of weight in the room. Following that instinct spared me from mistakes I might still be paying for. Other times, my gut told me to take a risk that seemed too big: establishing my first company while still studying, or rewriting a speech in ten minutes before going up on an international stage, and still delivering it beside the minister of labour. Logic might have told me to step back. My gut told me to step forward.

And then there were the small, almost uncanny moments. Once, I sat with a friend over lunch. I looked at his face and, without thinking, said: "Yes, it's good there are no flies while we eat." He froze and stared at me. "That's scary," he replied, "because I was just thinking that exact thing." That wasn't magic; it was the gut reading subtle cues—the shift in his gaze and the way his attention moved. It reminded me how much we pick up without words, and how intuition allows us to connect with others on a level deeper than speech.

The gut is not infallible; it must be tempered with reason and patience. But when aligned with discipline, it becomes a powerful guide. The lesson I've learned is this: if logic is the compass, gut feeling is the wind. Together, they can steer you forward. Alone, either can mislead.

In the silence of intuition, I found guidance that no mentor could give me. And by learning to trust it, I discovered a truth: often, the map we seek is already written inside us.

What we call "gut instinct" is really the brain's pattern-recognition system at work. The subconscious mind processes micro-signals—tiny shifts in facial muscles, changes in tone, even pauses in speech—far faster than conscious thought. Research shows that the ventromedial prefrontal cortex integrates these cues with past experiences, producing a felt sense of "something's off" or "this is right" long before the conscious brain explains why.

That is why you can look at a friend and sense their thoughts or walk into a room and feel if something is wrong. It is your nervous system decoding patterns beneath awareness. And when aligned with discipline and patience, this kind of intuition becomes a powerful, trustworthy guide.

Three Components of Your Inner Guide

If discipline gave me structure, patience gave me endurance, and gut feelings gave me direction, together they formed something I had lacked for most of my life: a compass I could trust.

Discipline was the daily anchor. It turned lofty goals into small, repeatable steps—reading another page, finishing another assignment, and showing up when I did not feel like it. Without discipline, everything would have collapsed under the weight of emotion or distraction.

Patience was the glue. Change rarely came as quickly as I wanted. There were long gaps between the release in 2017, the decision to go absolutist in 2019, and graduating from King's in 2025. Without patience, I would have quit during those silent years when results were invisible. Patience taught me that waiting is not wasted time—it is preparation.

Gut feeling was the silent guide. It told me when to cut ties with old circles, when to risk building companies, and when to step onto stages I thought were too big for me. Logic alone might have hesitated. Gut told me to move. Without it, I would have stayed in safe but stagnant places.

Each is incomplete on its own. Discipline without patience turns into burnout. Patience without gut turns into waiting forever. Gut without discipline leads to chaos. But woven together, they created a system I could live by—structured, enduring, and responsive to the silent signals life offers.

That balance became the foundation not only of my recovery but of everything I built afterward. It was no longer about running from the past. It was about walking forward with a compass steady enough to hold me on course.

Purpose is never found in a single moment of clarity. It begins as a quiet spark within—a sense that something must change—but it only becomes real when it is lived outward. That is where discipline, patience, and instinct meet. Discipline gives you the structure to stay the course. Patience gives you the endurance to keep walking when results feel far away. Gut feelings give you the direction, the inner compass that points you toward choices logic alone cannot always explain.

For me, these three became the scaffolding of a new life. They steadied me when temptation whispered. They carried me through years of study, long nights of work, and the leap into building businesses. They gave me the courage to trust my own instincts and the strength to stand by them.

But discipline, patience, and guts alone are not the whole story. They are tools, yes—but what gave them power was how they connected with my scars, my story, and my willingness to share. I began to see that my past was not just something to rise above; it could be a bridge, a way to reach others who were still lost where I once was.

That is where the next chapter begins: Your Story Is Your Bridge— how everything you have lived, even the darkest moments, can become the very thing that connects you to others and gives meaning to the journey.

CHAPTER 13

Your Story Is Your Bridge

Why Your Experience Matters More Than You Think

I remember sitting across from a friend one afternoon—just an ordinary lunch, nothing staged or formal. We were halfway through our meals when the conversation drifted toward life, choices, and the mess we sometimes make of both. I shared a piece of my journey—not the polished version, but the raw truth of prison, addiction, and the long climb back through education and business. I expected silence or maybe polite sympathy. Instead, he leaned back, looked me straight in the eyes, and said:

"You know these things because you have been at the bottom and have risen. That makes your story a success story."

The words landed harder than I expected. Success story? For years, I had thought of myself as the opposite: a man defined by mistakes, shame, and scars I believed were too deep to ever be worth anything. Yet here was someone telling me that the very scars I carried made me credible. My failures were not disqualifications, but evidence of survival.

I sat there with my fork in hand, the noise of the café fading for a moment. What struck me was not pride but responsibility. If my story had weight for him, maybe it could carry weight for others. Maybe the broken pieces I had once tried so hard to hide could actually become bridges. In that moment, I realized that the past I had wanted to bury was the very thing that made my voice matter.

For a long time, I believed my story didn't matter. Maybe you've felt the same—that your experiences are too messy, too broken, too unfinished to be worth sharing. Shame has a way of whispering that lie over and over until it feels like the truth. It tells you that because you stumbled, because you failed, because you carry scars, you are somehow disqualified from contributing anything meaningful.

That lie is powerful because it attaches itself to the most vulnerable places in us. When you are sitting alone with your regrets, shame convinces you that nobody could possibly understand, or worse, that if they knew, they would turn away. So you hide. You bury the memories, silence your voice, and pretend the weight does not exist. But the silence does not heal—it corrodes.

Here is the truth: struggle does not disqualify you. It qualifies you. And remember: what does not kill you makes you stronger.

When someone is lost in addiction, shame, or failure, they do not need a perfect guide who has never stumbled. They need someone who knows what it feels like to crawl through the mud and still get up. They need a voice that carries the weight of lived experience, not just theory. That is why your story matters more than you think.

The very things you believe make you unworthy may be the things that give you credibility. Scars prove you have survived. Setbacks prove you have stood back up. Pain proves you have lived, learned, and endured. Struggle does not diminish your story; it sharpens it.

The lie of insignificance thrives in silence. The truth of your story emerges when you dare to speak it.

For a long time, I believed my scars were only proof of failure. Prison was a mark of shame. Addiction was something to hide. Psychosis was a chapter I hoped no one would ever know. Even going back to high school at thirty-eight felt like a confession that I had wasted too much of my life.

But over time, I learned that the very things I thought disqualified me were the same things that gave me credibility. When I sit across from someone who feels like their life is broken beyond repair, I do not speak from theory. I speak from living it. I know what it feels like to wake up in a cell and wonder if life is over. I know what it is like to run on substances to silence the noise in my own head. And I know the grind of rebuilding from zero—page after page, problem after problem, course after course.

That lived experience became a language others could trust. People listen differently when you have been where they are. My story does not promise perfection—it proves possibility. It shows that scars are not barriers to connection; they are the bridges.

There is a reason lived experience has such power. Neuroscience shows that when we share stories, especially ones charged with emotion, they activate not only the language centers of the brain but also the empathy networks. Memory and emotion together light up the brain's mirror systems—the circuits that allow us to "feel" what someone else feels. This is why hearing theory can teach us, but hearing lived pain can move us. Our brains connect more deeply when truth comes from experience.

What I once tried to bury became the very tools I use to help others. Prison, addiction, psychosis, shame—they are not just part of my past; they are proof that falling doesn't mean staying down. My scars tell the truth in a way no textbook ever could: change is possible because I have lived it.

When people hear about my journey—prison, addiction, psychosis, rebuilding through education and business—they sometimes imagine that impact only comes from stages, conferences, or television screens. But here is the truth: the most powerful moments of impact in my life have not come under bright lights. They have come across simple tables, in quiet rooms, over cups of coffee.

I have sat with people carrying shame so heavy it bent their posture. I have listened to friends describe nights of restless thoughts, convinced no one could understand. More than once, someone has told me, "It feels easy to talk to you. Like a burden just lifted." That did not happen because I had a polished speech or the perfect advice. It happened because I was willing to be present, to be real, and to let my scars show.

Sometimes the bravest thing we can give another person is the reminder that they are not alone, and that change is possible through small, steady steps.

These are not dramatic headlines. They are quiet exchanges that leave ripples. And often, those ripples go further than we realize.

Not everyone is called to stand on an international stage. Not everyone needs to broadcast their story. But everyone has the chance to impact one person at a time. A word of honesty over lunch. A shared story in confidence. A moment of presence when someone feels invisible.

Authenticity matters more than perfection. People do not need to see a flawless life; they need to see a true one. Your story—ordinary as it may feel—might be exactly what someone else needs to hear to believe in their own tomorrow.

For years, I saw my past as proof that I was unworthy. Prison sentences, addictions, psychosis, failures in relationships—they all looked like stains that marked me permanently. Shame whispered that because of those scars, I could never belong among people who were steady, educated, or successful. I thought the past had written my future in ink.

But with time, I learned to see differently. The past does not disqualify you; it prepares you. Every failure, every scar, every night spent wondering if life was even worth it became part of the language I now speak. When I sit across from someone struggling with shame or self-destruction, I do not need a textbook to understand them. I have been there. That credibility does not come from theory—it comes from survival.

Scars are not stains. They are maps. They do not erase where you have been, but they point the way forward. A scar across the skin tells a story of healing, not just injury. The same is true for the heart and mind. Each scar carries evidence that you endured, that you made it through, and that you carry knowledge others might desperately need.

Reframing the past means refusing to see yourself only through the lens of regret. It means recognizing that what once weighed you down can now be the very bridge that helps someone else cross over despair.

Your story is not ruined by scars. They strengthen it. And what you carry—the pain, the lessons, the resilience—can become the lifeline another person needs. Do not hide your scars. They may be the exact map someone else is searching for.

Helping Others by Sharing Your Thoughts

I had already learned that mentorship is not only about speeches, advice, or grand gestures—it's often about showing up. Still, some moments remind you of that truth more powerfully than others.

Helping others is not a lecture; it's not advice—it is presence. Mentorship is often practical. It is not just about words but about actions. Sometimes it means simply standing beside someone in their moment of fear and carrying part of the weight for them.

Looking back, I realized again that people do not always need perfect answers. Often, what they need most is to know they are not alone. That day reminded me that being there, even in ordinary ways, can be the most powerful guidance of all.

People often imagine mentorship as something grand—polished speeches, perfect strategies, or big stages. But most of the time, what people truly need is simple: honesty spoken at the right moment, backed by action.

I once told someone close to me something she had felt but never dared to say out loud: "You are not in the environment where you belong." She was trapped in a violent and abusive relationship. Words alone would not save her, but honesty broke through the denial and gave her strength to face reality. I did not stop at saying it–I helped her empty her apartment, packed her things, and drove her to another city to start fresh. That was not a speech, not a theory, but presence in action. Sometimes the most honest words are paired with practical help, and together they become a turning point.

Another time, a friend wrote to me, thanking me for always being there–for defending her when she felt small, for standing by her when others walked away. She told me, "A real friend acts this way." For me, those moments felt natural–just doing what was right. But to her, they were proof that loyalty and truth-telling could make her feel safe again.

Here is the truth: words do not fix everything, but they open the door. And sometimes, they open it just wide enough for someone to find the courage to walk through. Never underestimate the power of your honesty. You do not need to be perfect, polished, or powerful to make a difference. You just need to speak the truth, and when possible, stand beside someone as they take their next step. That combination–honesty and presence–can be life-changing.

Mentorship and impact don't come in one form. They live on different platforms, from the quietest one-on-one conversations to the public stages lit by lights and cameras. What changes is the reach, but what stays the same is the essence: honesty and presence.

Some of the most powerful moments I have experienced happened in private. One-on-one mentoring has a unique intimacy. Sitting across from someone–whether in a café, during a walk, or late at night over the phone–I have seen how truth lands differently when there is no audience. When I told a friend she was not in the environment where she belonged and helped her move away from an abusive relationship, it was not just advice—it was shared courage. In those moments, the power is not in polished words but in presence. Someone feels less alone, and that can be enough to ignite a change.

Then there are small groups and teams. As I built companies, I discovered that leadership was not about speeches or slogans—it was about modeling consistency. Showing up on time. Doing the work you expect others to do. Holding yourself accountable before asking it from anyone else. People do not follow words; they follow patterns. And in small circles, your actions are magnified. They either reinforce trust or erode it.

On the other end of the spectrum are public platforms—conferences, interviews, media appearances. Speaking in Uzbekistan, sitting next to ministers, with cameras broadcasting, was a surreal moment for me. It was proof that a story born in the shadows could echo far beyond them. But even then, the principle was the same. The audience didn't need perfection; they needed honesty. They needed to know that scars can become strength.

**Me and Bekhzod Musaev, Minister of
Employment and Poverty Reduction of Uzbekistan.**

The contrast between these platforms is real. A coffee table talk may deeply touch one's life. A television broadcast may ripple across millions. Yet the heart of impact is the same—it is not about the scale; it is about the truth behind the words and being present at the moment. People do not remember polished speeches as much as they remember when someone showed up real, unguarded, and present.

That is the secret: whether face-to-face, with a team, or on a stage, the power is not in performance but in presence.

Looking back, the biggest transformation wasn't just the platforms I spoke on—it was the man who stood on them. Years ago, I hid behind masks, bravado, and noise, terrified of anyone seeing the truth. Now, whether I sit across from one person in pain, guide a small team, or step onto an international stage, I no longer need to perform. I only need to be present.

That shift is the real story. Impact is not about being the loudest voice in the room. It is about showing up honestly, with scars visible and lessons intact. My younger self would have chased recognition; today, I chase connection. And in every platform—from a coffee table to a conference hall—that is what truly changes lives.

The Power Within a Story

When we share our story honestly, something powerful happens in the brain—for both the listener and the speaker.

For the listener, stories activate mirror neurons, the cells in the brain that allow us to "feel with" someone else. This is why when you hear about someone's pain or triumph, you do not just understand it—you experience a shadow of it yourself. That is empathy, written into our biology. It is also why even a quiet, personal story can create a connection faster than any lecture or advice.

Honest storytelling also triggers the release of oxytocin, sometimes called the "bonding hormone." Oxytocin lowers defensiveness and increases trust. When someone hears a vulnerable truth—like shame, loss, or recovery—their brain moves from isolation toward connection. That is why people often say, "A weight lifted," after opening up. The biology of trust has been engaged.

For the speaker, telling the story matters just as much. Traumatic memories are often stored in the amygdala, the brain's alarm center. They sit there, raw and overwhelming. But when we retell and reframe them, especially in safe contexts, those same memories are re-encoded through the prefrontal cortex. That process reduces their sting and builds resilience. The brain literally learns: this pain no longer controls me; it can serve me.

And empathy is not just between people. Anyone who has ever had a dog knows this. Dogs read our faces, mirror our emotions, and respond with connection. Neuroscience confirms that this bond also releases oxytocin, proving that empathy can be forged even beyond human-to-human contact.

Me in negotiations with clients.

Takeaway: Your story matters not only emotionally but biologically. Every time you share it, you are not just inspiring someone—you are helping rewire both their brain and your own for connection, resilience, and growth.

Sharing your story is never a one-way street. On the surface, it looks like service—giving hope, offering perspective, opening a door for someone else. But the truth is, every time you speak, write, or sit across from a person who is struggling, you are also holding yourself accountable.

When I began sharing honestly about my journey—prison, addiction, rebuilding, education—I felt the weight of my own words. If I stood in front of someone and told them that change was possible, that discipline mattered, that consistency builds trust, then I had no choice but to live that myself. Sharing became a mirror. It reflected not only what I had done but what I still needed to do to stay true.

This accountability is what sustains growth. Temptations, setbacks, and fatigue still come, but the memory of someone's eyes lighting up when they realize they are not alone—that keeps me steady. The responsibility to model resilience is not a burden; it is fuel.

And here is the most important part: legacy is not built on the size of the audience but on the consistency of impact. Some days, it was a media interview reaching millions. Other days, it was driving a friend to the hospital or helping someone pack their things to escape an abusive home. Both mattered equally. Both carried the same principle: presence + honesty = impact.

Sharing sustains you because it keeps you honest, grounded, and aligned with the person you have fought to become. It turns scars into service—not once, but every single time you speak.

Your story is not yours to hoard. The voice you carry, the scars you have turned into words, the lessons you have carved out of pain—they are not just for you. They are a bridge. Somewhere, someone is standing in the same silence you once knew, convinced they are broken, convinced there is no way forward. For them, your voice can be the proof that survival is possible, that transformation is real.

I used to believe my story was nothing but wreckage—prison records, addictions, shameful chapters that only proved failure. Now I see differently. Each scar is a map, and each word spoken from it can light the path for someone else. When I sat with people one-on-one, spoke in rooms filled with leaders, or appeared before audiences of millions, the impact was never about numbers. It was always about connection—one life touching another.

But here is the hidden truth: giving my story away has sustained me as much as it has helped others. Each time I speak, I recommit to the life I have built. Each time I mentor, I am reminded of the discipline and honesty I must keep. Sharing is not only a service—it is accountability.

So, remember this: your voice is not for you alone. It is the bridge someone else needs to cross.

But here is the thing—every bridge has a starting point. Every story of transformation begins with a spark. For me, it was not dramatic fireworks, but something quieter: a moment when the smallest decision lit the path forward.

And that's where we go next: Chapter 14—The Spark That Starts It All.

The Spark That Starts It All

Why Self-Motivation Is Everything

The first nights after my release were the quietest of my life. No guards, no locked doors, no footsteps echoing down a corridor. Just me, a small desk, and a hill of textbooks waiting like silent judges. High school courses and notes I had carried out of prison—all of it stared back at me. There was no teacher in the next room, no classmates, no one to remind me of deadlines. And there was no cheerleader to clap me forward.

It was freedom, yes—but freedom with weight. I realized quickly that no one was going to drag me forward. If I wanted to keep the promise I had made to myself inside those prison walls, the drive had to come from me. Alone in that room, I felt exposed and responsible.

The temptation to drift was strong. After all, who would notice if I did not open the math book? Who would care if I put the essays aside for tomorrow? But I knew the truth: if I did not move, no one would move me. And if I slipped, no one would stop me.

What empowered me in that moment were two things: big dreams and the hunger for a better life. I could see flashes of what might be possible—education, business, freedom built on my own terms. And behind those dreams was something deeper: that internal fire called sisu that I had carried all my life.

So I opened the first book. I forced my eyes over the first page. It was not glorious; it was slow, frustrating, and humbling. But that night, I understood something that has never left me: motivation would not fall from the sky. It had to be built from the inside out.

Isolation gave me responsibility. Responsibility gave me empowerment. And empowerment lit the first spark.

Many people live under the illusion that motivation will one day arrive like a spark—sudden, electrifying, undeniable. They wait for the "right time," the "right mood," or for some magical surge of energy to carry them forward. But waiting for motivation is one of the biggest traps there is. If you sit around waiting to feel ready, you may never take the first step.

The truth is simple but hard to accept: motivation is not what starts the journey—it is what grows because you have already started. Action builds motivation, not the other way around.

I remember this lesson vividly when I sat down in my prison cell with my first math test. The paper was in front of me, the pen cold in my hand. Did I feel ready? Absolutely not. My mind was full of doubts: It has been years. You are too old. What if you fail? The temptation was to wait—to wait for more confidence, more clarity, more of that elusive "motivation."

But waiting would have given me nothing, so I picked up the pen and started. The numbers on the page looked strange at first, almost mocking, but with each problem I attempted, something shifted. By the time I had finished the test, I did not just have answers on paper; I had proof that I could still learn. That proof sparked motivation in a way that sitting idle never could.

Motivation, I discovered, is like fire. You do not stand around waiting for it to light itself; you strike the match, you gather kindling, you build it piece by piece. And only then does the fire grow.

If you are waiting for the perfect wave of inspiration, stop. Take the step. Do the work. The feeling will follow.

Self-Motivation Is a Commitment

Self-motivation is not built on hype or quick bursts of energy. It is built on self-discipline—the quiet, often boring commitment to do the right thing over and over again, long after the initial excitement fades. Motivation might get you started, but only discipline keeps you moving when nothing feels exciting at all.

In prison, and later after release, I had to learn this truth firsthand. There was no teacher standing over me, no boss checking whether I opened my books. If I wanted to finish high school, I had to set my own structure: mornings for Swedish and math, afternoons for essays, evenings for review and work in the middle. When I stepped into freedom, the routine did not magically get easier. The outside world was full of noise and temptation, but I kept the same discipline. Day by day, page by page, I built momentum.

The key was setting goals that I could actually reach. First, pass one test. Then, finish a course. Then, complete the term. Each mid-goal gave me a sense of progress, a reason to keep going. Without those milestones, the long road would have felt impossible. Discipline taught me to break the impossible down into small, manageable victories.

Self-discipline is like tending a fire. You do not light it once and expect it to burn forever. You add wood, adjust the flames, and keep feeding it daily. If you neglect it, the fire dies out. But if you return to it consistently, even on the coldest days, it keeps you warm and alive.

And behind that discipline, there was something deeper: *sisu*. The Finnish word does not translate perfectly, but it captures a kind of raw willpower, a refusal to quit even when strength has already run out. It is a core part of Finnish national identity, associated with courage, perseverance, and the ability to accomplish tasks that seem impossible.

The paradox of *sisu* is that it is not about brute force; it is about accepting that there will be pain, fatigue, and loneliness, and choosing to keep moving anyway. When I accepted that truth, I stopped wasting energy resisting hardship. Instead, I leaned into it, letting sisu carry me forward. For this word meant one thing above all: giving up is never an option.

That is the role of discipline—and *sisu*—in change. It is not exactly thrilling, but it is powerful. It turns dreams into plans and plans into results—step by step, goal by goal, day after day. And once you commit to it fully, giving up is no longer even on the table.

I have to accept that reality is not forged in dramatic victories; the long grind means I was not just studying but also working to serve my future self. The nature of *sisu* is quiet. It does not shout. It does not arrive with fanfare. Days often stretched from early mornings at work to late nights with textbooks spread across the table. There was no luxury of choosing one path; both demanded everything. In those moments, motivation was not enough, and even discipline felt mechanical. What carried me forward was the unshakable conviction that giving up was never an option.

Looking back, *sisu* was the bridge between decision and result. Deciding to change in 2016 was powerful. Graduating from King's was rewarding. But what carried me across the years of study, work, and relentless grind was *sisu*—that quiet insistence that no matter how heavy the day felt, I would not quit.

That is the depth of *sisu*: not a dramatic burst, but a steady fire. A lifelong commitment to endure, adapt, and build, even when every excuse to stop is right in front of you.

Cultivating the Drive for Success

Self-motivation is often portrayed as an inner flame that some people have and others do not. *But neuroscience shows a different story: motivation is not a gift; it is a process. It is less about waiting for inspiration and more about building systems inside the brain that reinforce effort with reward.*

At the center of this process is dopamine, the neurotransmitter often linked to pleasure. But dopamine isn't just about the high of achievement; it is about anticipation and reinforcement. Every time you complete a small task, your brain releases dopamine, rewarding the action and making you more likely to repeat it. In other words, motivation grows by doing, not by waiting to feel ready.

For me, this principle became clear in the smallest victories: Finishing a single math assignment in prison, completing a Swedish test; later, after release, submitting an essay at the University of Eastern Finland after a long workday. None of these moments was life-changing in itself, but each one left a trace in my brain—proof that effort leads to progress. Neuroscience calls this building new neural pathways. I call it building a "proof bank." Every time I pushed through resistance and finished a task, I deposited evidence that I could do it again.

Over time, those deposits added up. The brain thrives on patterns, and the cycle of action → small win → dopamine reward → more action creates momentum. Instead of chasing chaos-driven dopamine highs—the quick hits from alcohol, substances, or reckless living—my brain slowly rewired itself to crave the quieter, steadier rewards of progress. The same system that once trapped me in destructive loops now sustained me in constructive ones.

This shift does not happen overnight. In the early days, my old brain patterns screamed for shortcuts: escape the boredom, numb the anxiety, find something fast. But each time I chose to stay, to finish, to persist, I was reshaping the circuits of my mind. I experienced the process of neuroplasticity as discipline turned into motivation, and motivation turned into vision.

Looking back, the process is simple but profound: action creates motivation, not the other way around. Small steps—even the ones that feel insignificant—send signals to the brain that change is possible. And when those signals accumulate, they build a new identity: someone who does not just dream of change but lives it.

What also mattered was my nature. I have never been afraid to fail. Failure, to me, was feedback, data that showed me what did not work. That fearless relationship with setbacks worked in harmony with the science. The brain encodes failure as strongly as success, but when you interpret it with optimism, it becomes fuel rather than shame. My optimism was not naïve cheerfulness; it was a principle. I chose to believe that tomorrow could be better, that effort could compound, and that one step forward mattered even when the horizon was far away.

For me, optimism and principles were like a compass. Even when storms hit, even when progress was painfully slow, the compass kept pointing forward. I did not always know how far the journey would take me, but I trusted that as long as I kept walking—with discipline, patience, and *sisu*—the direction was right. That compass, paired with the brain's ability to rewire itself, turned motivation from something fragile into something unbreakable.

It is the same system that carried me from solving a math test in prison at thirty-eight to standing years later as a Master of Laws in London. The principle never changed: act first, and motivation will follow.

Self-motivation is everything. At the end of the day, no mentor, no system, no second chance will carry you forward if you do not choose to move your own feet. People can encourage you; they can open doors; they can even walk beside you for a time. But no one else can live your story for you. That responsibility—and that privilege—will always rest in your hands.

I learned this sitting at a desk with nothing but books, tired eyes, and silence. I learned it by working shifts while studying, setting goals when no one else was keeping score. I learned it when I made the decision in 2016 to turn my life from night to day—no excuses, no way back. After the decision, every choice was a spark. But a spark is not enough unless you feed it daily.

That is what self-motivation really is: the steady, relentless tending of a fire that will go out if you neglect it. Not dramatic, not glamorous—just daily. And the truth is, once you light that fire, you must keep it alive every day after.

But here is the greater question: once you know how to spark yourself, how do you pass that flame forward? Because true growth does not end with you. It grows when you light a spark in others.

That is the next step—how to ignite hope, determination, and vision in the people around you. The way you build self-motivation through action before inspiration will become the foundation for showing others how to light their own spark.

How to Light the Spark in Others

It was not in a boardroom or on a stage. It was over an ordinary lunch. A friend had been struggling—restless, weighed down, unsure how to move forward. He asked me, casually: "How did you do it?"

I did not launch into a speech. I did not give him a list of steps. I told him the truth: "I made a decision. Then I committed to it. Every day—with *sisu*, determination, and consistency."

He grew quiet, letting the words settle. Finally, he said, "That is it, isn't it? Not magic. Just decision and persistence." And in his eyes, I saw it—the spark. Not because I told him what to do, but because he saw that I was living it.

That is when I understood something essential: you cannot talk someone into change. You can only light the spark by living your truth in front of them. My discipline, my sobriety, my education, my businesses—they were more than milestones. They became mirrors that showed others what was possible for them too.

Motivation is contagious, but not in the way many people imagine. It does not spread through speeches or hype; it spreads through quiet, visible consistency. People believe in what they can see, not just what they hear. That is why living your principles every day is the strongest way to light a spark in others.

I have seen this many times. A friend once told me, "It's not what you say that inspires me, it's that you do the same thing every single day." What he was noticing was not dramatic achievements—it was the discipline of steady action. Whether it was finishing courses, showing up to work while studying, or committing to routines even when no one was watching, consistency was the proof.

But consistency without honesty is just performance. What made the difference in my journey was that I did not pretend it was easy. I did not hide the long nights, the setbacks, or the moments of doubt. When people saw me balancing study, work, and building businesses, they did not see perfection—they saw persistence. They saw someone who kept moving forward without sugarcoating the struggle. That honesty gave my actions weight. It showed that success was not about being flawless, but about being faithful to the process.

When I came out of prison and sat at my desk with textbooks and assignments, there was no teacher reminding me to stay focused. No mentor checking if I stayed on track. The only accountability was me. But over time, those who watched from the outside—family, colleagues, even strangers—began to notice. They saw someone who did not quit, someone who lived what he said. That, more than any words, gave them permission to believe they could keep going too.

The truth is that consistency is magnetic, but only when it is real. When you live with honesty and discipline long enough, others want to know how. They catch fire not because you told them to, but because you showed them what is possible. And once they see it lived out, they can no longer tell themselves it is impossible.

There's a unique kind of energy that comes when people realize they are part of something bigger than themselves. For years, my life was only about me—my next move, my next escape, my next high. That tunnel vision kept me small. But when I began building companies, mentoring people, and stepping into international projects, I discovered something different: vision is one of the most powerful sparks you can pass on.

I have seen it in small rooms and in big ones. A young employee, unsure of his place, suddenly lit up when I explained that the work we were doing wasn't just about business—it was about building stability and opportunities for others. He began to see that his role mattered. What might have felt like just another job turned into part of a mission. That shift—from task to purpose—changed the way he carried himself.

I saw the same spark during international projects. In Uzbekistan, while sitting with leaders and decision-makers, I realized that agreements were not just contracts on paper; they were bridges connecting people and creating opportunities across borders. The people around me could feel it too. They were not just negotiating terms; they were participating in something that could shape lives on a larger scale. That sense of shared vision lifted the atmosphere.

The truth is, people often search for a reason to push beyond their limits. Alone, motivation fades. But when they are part of a bigger picture—when they feel their actions connect to something lasting—their energy multiplies. Shared vision gives meaning to sacrifice, endurance, and effort.

For me, lighting that spark meant not only painting the picture but also living it out. People will only believe in a vision if they can trust the person who carries it. That is why consistency, honesty, and persistence matter—they make the vision credible. Without them, words are just words.

What I have learned is this: when you invite people into a vision, you are not only helping them build something external, but you are also helping them discover new strength within themselves. They stop asking, "Why should I bother?" and start saying, "This matters." That is when the spark catches fire.

Looking back, I see now that the greatest influence I have ever had was not through perfect speeches, polished words, or carefully designed strategies. It was through showing up–honestly, consistently, and imperfectly human.

When I rebuilt my life brick by brick, people did not just see the results. They saw the process. They saw the nights of study, the routines I refused to abandon, the choices to stay sober, to stay steady, to stay moving forward even when progress felt invisible. And in that process, their own sparks began to catch.

That is the essence of lighting a fire in others. You do not hand them your flame; you remind them they already carry their own. Through presence, through action, and through honesty, you give them permission to believe again. Neuroscience explains it with mirror neurons and oxytocin, but in the end, it is much simpler: hope is contagious.

For me, sharing my story was never just about service. It was accountability. Each time I spoke, each time someone looked to me for strength, I had to recommit. I could not live in two stories. I had to keep aligning my words with my actions. And in that alignment, my purpose deepened.

Here is the truth I want you to take with you: your story is not yours alone. It is a bridge. Every scar, every setback, every triumph you have lived has the power to become someone else's roadmap. Do not underestimate it. Do not hide it. Share it.

Because this–this moment of giving back, of sparking others– is not the end of your journey. It is only the beginning. Which is exactly where the next chapter begins: **This Is not the End–It Is the Beginning.**

CHAPTER 15

This Is Not the End—It Is the Beginning

What Happens When Purpose Meets Action

The first thing I notice these days is the quiet. Sitting in my home office, coffee steaming beside me, the screen lights up with the day's first remote meeting. A team member is dialing in from another city, a client from another country. Plans are reviewed, ideas exchanged, progress made. It is efficient, purposeful, and calm.

What strikes me most, though, is not the technology or the reach—it is the peace of mind. That is something money cannot buy. And in my past life, it was something I could never hold on to. Back then, silence was unbearable. My head was full of noise, my body restless with chaos, and peace felt like an illusion I would never grasp.

Now, the quiet is not my enemy; it is the foundation. Instead of waking up to regret or the scramble of survival, I wake up to a rhythm built on purpose. The businesses I run, the partnerships I manage, the people who depend on me—all of it flows from choices made years ago, when I sat in a cell with nothing but books, stubbornness, and the belief that something else was possible.

It is naturally tedious. There are no fireworks in the daily grind of emails, calls, and steady planning. But there is something extraordinary in the ordinary: a life no longer dictated by chaos but by intention. This peace of mind, this ability to act with clarity, is what happens when purpose finally meets action.

Before, my life was full of action without purpose. I was always busy, always chasing, but nothing I did was lasting. Chaos disguised itself as momentum. I lived in noise, not direction. And in that noise, peace of mind was impossible.

There is a difference between knowing what you want and actually building it. Purpose without action is only a dream. Action without purpose is only noise. It's when the two come together that transformation begins. Many people know what they want—freedom, growth, stability—but stop short of acting on it.

A dream left untouched begins to feel like a burden. I knew that if I wanted change, I could not only dream about it. I had to move.

So I chose goals and committed to walking toward them step by step. First, high school, then university, then business ventures. Each action, no matter how small, was tied to something larger. That connection created a kind of calm I had never known before. I did not need to rush or chase anymore. I just needed to keep moving toward the goals I had set.

That is the real power: when purpose fuels action, restlessness fades. You no longer live in noise or drift in uncertainty—instead, every step matters. Peace of mind does not come from having everything—it comes from knowing that what you do today is leading you somewhere you have chosen.

One of the most powerful lessons I've learned is that momentum compounds. Just like interest in a bank account, small actions aligned with a bigger purpose stack up over time until they become something far greater than the sum of their parts.

Nothing in my story came from a single "big break." No lightning bolt transformed my life overnight. Instead, it was small, steady, sometimes quiet actions that began to layer on top of each other.

Finishing high school at forty was not glamorous. But that foundation opened the door to the University of Eastern Finland, which, step by step, led to King's College London. None of those stages happened instantly—they were built by showing up daily, even when tired, even when progress felt slow.

The same principle applies to entrepreneurship. My first company was modest, but it proved I could create rather than destroy. From there came ventures that gave me greater competence, confidence, and impact.

And eventually, those steady steps carried me far beyond what I once imagined possible: into international forums and taking part in conversations that shaped real outcomes. None of it was a sudden leap; it was the result of thousands of small, deliberate actions compounded over years. Each decision to stay consistent, each effort to keep moving forward, was layered into opportunities that connected me with professionals across the world. What began as discipline turned into networks, and what began as networks often grew into genuine friendships—bonds built on shared values and respect rather than chaos and noise.

Momentum has its own kind of peace. When your actions align with your goals, you do not need to force breakthroughs or chase shortcuts. You know that each step adds to the whole. Even when progress feels invisible, the compounding effect is working in the background, stacking one choice on top of another until the results become undeniable.

Looking back, I can see clearly: my life did not change because of one big moment. It changed because I learned to trust the compound effect of aligned actions. Peace of mind came not from speed, but from knowing that consistency would eventually create results bigger than anything I could see in the moment.

There was a time when I lived like a leaf in the wind—drifting, reacting, pushed by every gust of circumstance. If something felt heavy, I ran. If a new distraction appeared, I followed. Without purpose, there was no anchor. My identity shifted depending on the room, the company, or the substance in my system. I wasn't grounded. I was reactive, defined by chaos.

Purpose changed that. It did not erase storms–life still brings setbacks, losses, and challenges–but it gave me something stable to stand on when the winds came. When I committed to education, business, and sobriety, those were not just external goals; they became anchors. I was not the man chasing relief anymore–I was the man building. And when your life is rooted in purpose, setbacks do not uproot you. They test you, yes, but they no longer define you.

This is more than philosophy–neuroscience backs it. Purpose engages the brain's reward circuits in a way that is deeper and longer-lasting than quick highs. Substances, chaos, and distractions give you short dopamine spikes that crash almost as fast as they rise. Purpose, however, links effort to meaning. Each small action aligned with purpose releases dopamine in a steadier rhythm, creating what scientists call "sustainable motivation." Over time, your brain literally learns to prefer the steady rewards of building over the fleeting hits of escape.

For me, this rewiring showed up in daily life. Where once I would have spiralled in anxiety or shame, now I could say: I have work to do. I have goals that matter. That grounding gave me peace of mind–something no drug, no muscle, no bravado ever delivered.

And storms, instead of being proof that I was lost, became training grounds. After all, smooth seas do not forge strong sailors. It was the rough waters that taught me resilience, patience, and the steadiness of purpose.

Purpose stabilized my identity. I was no longer just a survivor of storms. I became a builder who could endure them–and even grow stronger because of them.

Purpose is about planting seeds that will grow long after I am gone. For years, my life was about instant gratification, about chasing highs that vanished the moment they arrived. Now, the satisfaction comes from knowing that what I build today creates ripples tomorrow. A company does not just exist for me; it becomes a platform for others to work, to grow, and to find stability. A conversation over coffee does not just relieve a burden in the moment—it can change how someone sees themselves, and through them, how they raise their children, lead their teams, or treat their communities.

This is the difference between a life consumed by chaos and a life driven by purpose. Chaos collapses in on itself; purpose expands outward. Each action aligned with purpose is like a stone dropped into water—the first splash may seem small, but the ripples carry further than you can track.

I often think about how my scars, once private battles I wanted to hide, now serve as maps others can use to navigate their own storms. That is the essence of legacy: not wealth, not titles, not recognition, but the quiet knowledge that something you did, said, or built continues to live in someone else's story.

Looking forward, I see life not as a closed circle but as an open horizon. The ripple effect of education, entrepreneurship, and mentoring will carry further than I can predict. And that is enough. I do not need to control where the waves land—I only need to keep throwing the stones of purpose into the water.

Because in the end, purpose plus action is not about me at all. It is about the continuum—a current stronger than any one life, moving forward, carrying stories, skills, and sparks into places I may never set foot. And that thought brings both humility and peace.

An Invitation to Step into Your New Life

The surface of Lake Pyhäjärvi was calm—a sheet of silver stretching out under the soft light of evening. I sat on the shore, surrounded by a kind of stillness that once would have felt unbearable. In the past, silence was a prison of its own: a space where my thoughts grew loud and restless, where I longed for noise, distraction—anything to escape myself.

But this night was different. I listened to the quiet, and instead of fear, I felt peace. The air carried the smell of water and pine, the horizon seemed endless, and I realized how much had changed within me. Stillness no longer meant confinement—it meant expansion. It meant the freedom to breathe, to imagine, and to let the past rest where it belonged.

Watching the ripples move slowly across the lake, I thought about how life itself works the same way. One choice, one act of courage, one refusal to quit—each creates ripples that spread far beyond what we can see. My own story, once bound by bars and shame, has grown into something I could never have predicted: education, business, mentoring, and a sense of peace that money cannot buy.

The lake reminded me of the horizon still ahead. Just as the water stretched out farther than my eyes could follow, so too did the impact of my actions, reaching into lives and futures I might never meet. And for the first time, that thought did not weigh me down—it lifted me.

There comes a point when reading, listening, or even dreaming is no longer enough. Stories can inspire, yes—but inspiration without action fades like smoke. I know this because I spent years consuming ideas, promising myself "tomorrow" would be different, only to find myself trapped in the same cycle. Change did not begin when I read about it; change began when I acted on it.

If you are reading these words now, I want you to understand something clearly: you are next. My story is not here to impress you, but to remind you that transformation is possible. Not easy, not quick—but possible. What I have achieved is not the product of luck, privilege, or chance. It is the result of decisions, repeated daily, even when no one was watching.

The act of opening reading materials in a solitary cell was not a grand revelation. No one cheered. No spotlight shone on me. But those small acts were sparks. They were me saying to myself, "I will not stay the same." And that's how momentum begins—not with applause, but with commitment.

You do not need to have the whole plan. You do not need to know how it will all unfold. You only need to take the first step and repeat it. That is the bridge between inspiration and transformation: action.

My story is proof not that the road is smooth, but that it is real. And if I could walk it from where I began, then you can too. The question is no longer, "Can I?" The question is, "Will I?"

Because the world does not just need you to read, the world needs you to rise.

There comes a point when inspiration must turn into movement. You have read my story; you have seen the transformation—but the question is not about me anymore. It is about you.

Laying Down the Foundation

Finding direction does not begin with grand gestures. It starts with simple anchors, like laying the first bricks of a foundation. Think of your life as a house under construction: values are the blueprint, daily actions are the bricks, and discipline is the mortar that holds it together. Without these, the structure does not stand.

Here is what I have learned, broken down so you can carry it forward:

1. **Define your compass.** Write down three values that you want your life to point toward. They do not need to be fancy—honesty, perseverance, or family can be enough. When storms come, these values will be the stars you navigate by.

2. **Take one step today.** Do not wait for the right moment. There will never be perfect conditions. Pick a single action aligned with your values—read a page, send an application, write down a goal—and do it. One step builds momentum.

3. **Build the rhythm.** Discipline is not about force; it is about rhythm. Just as waves keep shaping the shoreline, your repeated actions, small but steady, will carve out lasting change.

4. **Turn scars into tools.** Every mistake, every failure, every painful chapter is not wasted. They are not stains on your record—they are maps showing where not to return, and where you have the strength to guide others.

I remember filling out my first company registration papers while still grinding through my studies. The forms were long, the process uncertain, and my doubts loud. Around the same time, I submitted my application to the University of Eastern Finland. Neither step felt life-changing in the moment—they were just pieces of paper, sent off quietly. But those papers carried a decision: that I would no longer drift, I would build. Looking back, those small actions were sparks that lit fires I am still tending today.

Graduated from University of Eastern Finland.

Graduated from King's College

The Royal Festival Hall

Do not wait for someone else to hand you permission. Do not wait for clarity to arrive fully formed. The spark is already inside you. Light it, feed it with small daily acts, and watch it grow into something that carries you far beyond what you can see today.

This is your invitation. Your bridge. Your first brick. The world is not waiting for perfection—it is waiting for you to begin.

Dear Friend,

If you have walked with me through these pages, you have already proven something important: you are searching. And if you are searching, it means you have not given up. That, in itself, is strength.

I want you to know this—nothing in your story disqualifies you. Not the scars, not the shame, not the setbacks. What you see as failure may, in fact, be the foundation you are standing on to rise higher than you thought possible. I once believed I was finished—psychosis, addiction, prison, broken relationships. Yet those very scars became the tools that now allow me to build, to lead, to mentor, and to dream.

The truth is simple: no one else can live your story for you. No one else can carry your discipline or your next step. You can have mentors, friends, even cheerleaders, but in the end, it is your decision that lights the spark. And when that spark catches, it will illuminate not just your path but the paths of others who are watching—often in silence—waiting for proof that change is possible.

Do not wait for perfect timing. Do not wait until you feel ready. Start where you are, with what you have. Define your values. Take one step today. Build your rhythm. Let your scars speak not as reminders of where you fell, but as evidence of how you rose.

And when doubt comes—because it will—remember that discipline, patience, and honesty will always carry you farther than fleeting motivation ever could. I've walked that road, and if my story tells you anything, let it be this: transformation is not a miracle. It is a series of small, stubborn choices made day after day.

You are not broken. You are becoming. You are not late. You are right on time.

This is not the end of my story, or yours. This is the beginning. The rest is waiting for you to write.

With respect and belief in you,
Jani

Your audience deserves more than motivation –
they deserve transformation.

Scan to bring Jani's story to your stage.

About the Author

Jani Havunen is an accomplished legal and business advisor with deep expertise in corporate and commercial law, taxation, and international business. Holding an LL.M. in International Corporate and Commercial Law from King's College London and a master's degree in administrative sciences from the University of Eastern Finland, Jani combines rigorous legal insight with strategic business acumen.

As founder and CEO of multiple companies spanning legal services, personnel solutions, construction, and real estate investment, Jani has built a career at the intersection of law and enterprise. He is known for guiding organizations through complex regulatory landscapes and helping them achieve sustainable growth both in Finland and abroad.

Through his firm, Havunen Consulting, he provides tailored advisory services in taxation, business, and compliance, while his leadership roles at Smart Workers Ltd, Havurax Ltd, and BCI Apartments reflect his entrepreneurial drive and commitment to innovation.

Beyond his professional endeavors, Jani is passionate about continuous learning, international collaboration, and the evolving relationship between business freedom and regulatory frameworks—a theme he explores in his academic research on money laundering laws and constitutional rights.